Phonics Pra[...] Made Easy and Fun

Frustration-free method of teaching reading to new or struggling readers

Student Workbook A

Janis Dana

Acknowledgments
The author gratefully acknowledges the contributions and encouragement
of the following individuals in the completion of this project:
Editorial: Marilee McLeod, Gail Crowley
Project Management Assistance: Kiah Dana
Cover Design Assistance: Ryan Tilly
Love and Support: Michael Dana

**Dedicated to the hundreds of children who delighted me as they learned
to read. It is a privilege to continue teaching through these workbooks.**

Table of Contents

*   Short ea (as in br**ea**d) is in Workbook B
**   ie (as in n**ie**ce) and ei / eigh (as in dec**ei**t and **eigh**t) are in Workbook B
***   ow (as in **ow**l) is in Workbook B
****   ch (as in **Ch**ris and **ch**ef) is in Workbook B

Getting Started

- This is the first of two workbooks practicing 73 of the most common phonetic sounds of the English language. Workbook A is very basic, focusing on short and long vowels, consonant digraphs, and r-controlled vowels. Workbook B continues practice with other frequently encountered phonetic spellings and sounds. (See last page for list of sounds.)

- To ensure confidence from the start, begin only after students associate most consonants with their corresponding sounds. For adults who might need a refresher with these sounds, YouTube can help.

- **Each page of *Phonics Practice Made Easy and Fun* is designed to minimize distractions and allow the learner to focus on just one sound at a time.** Therefore, **sight words have been kept to a bare minimum.** The *only* sight words found on any of the short and long vowel pages are: is, the, do, to, he, be, me, we, has, his, are, go, no, old, of. These words, along with a few soundable words encountered before being formally introduced (yes, it, in, on, did, if, not, for, with), should ideally be taught ahead of time, before the student is assigned the page. For your convenience, any sight or extra-soundable words found on short or long vowel worksheets are listed at the bottom of each page.

- Teach each targeted phonetic sound clearly, both verbally and in print. In the beginning, and for as long as a student needs the support, help him or her sound out and blend actual words from the worksheet containing the focus sound before starting the page. (Write them on a whiteboard or make flashcards with index cards.)

- **To keep a child from being distracted by ever-changing directions and to instill a feeling of confidence, there are only two basic formats in the worktext—and kids *love* doing them!** Before allowing independent work, walk students through lessons of both formats, teaching how to think through answers according to the directions. Do this until children thoroughly understand what they are to do.

- **Important:** Let each child freely choose two or three colors (other than black or brown) with which to complete assigned pages, thus making every page a creative expression unique to each student. It's amazing how motivating this is. Stickers or stampers may also be used for variety. If a child makes a mistake, let him X out the wrong answer and color in the right one without penalty.

- After short and long vowels, lessons can be used in order, or pick and choose to match any reading program. Faster learners will use fewer pages. Note: More multi-syllabic words will be encountered in advanced segments, particularly in Middles and Endings.

- Use the **FIND AND FIX** feature when correcting to help prevent students from hurrying through their work without consequence for wrong answers and to provide excellent additional practice. When checking, do not mark *any wrong* on the page. Simply count the number of missed answers and record in the FIND AND FIX blank at the top left hand corner of the page. A child is then responsible for reading again through the entire page to find and fix that number of wrong answers. After doing this, if answers are still incorrect, reteach the sound and monitor the child's sounding and blending.

- Check-ups are provided after each sound or sound grouping.

- Helpful hint: Review previously practiced sounds frequently (even daily) by "chanting" their spellings and sounds with the following rhythm:
  Example for the "sh" spelling: Say the letter names "s" and "h" twice, then the sound three times: s - h, s – h, /sh/, /sh/, /sh/. This can be done with all the letter combinations. Great technique for cementing each sound and spelling into the mind.

Name_____

Directions for the student: **Practice reading 30 short a words on this page**. Choose 2-3 colors. Color **yes** if the sentence makes sense or could possibly be true. Color **no** if it does not make sense or could not be true.

1. Sam had a fat cat. | yes | no |

2. Ann is a bad man. | yes | no |

3. The hat ran fast. | yes | no |

4. A pan had ham in it. | yes | no |

5. The man had a nap. | yes | no |

6. Dan and Al sat. | yes | no |

7. Jam is in the fan. | yes | no |

8. An ant had a cap. | yes | no |

9. A bag is in the van. | yes | no |

10. A dad is a man. | yes | no |

Sight words: no is the / yes in it   1

Name_____

Directions for the student: **Practice reading 40 short a words on this page.** Choose 2-3 colors. Read each sentence or phrase. Pick the best answer and color it.

1. Dan can do it.

add	bag

2. Ann can pass it.

ham	pat

3. It ran fast.

rat	fat

4. In a van

tag	gas

5. In Sam's hand

bag	bad

6. Al sat in it.

sad	van

7. Jan had it.

jam	wag

8. Dad can do it.

hat	clap

9. The last man

Sam	can

10. Pam's dad

cat	Dan

2   Sight words: do to is the / it in

Name_____

Directions for the student: **Practice reading 28 short a words on this page.** Choose 2-3 colors. Color **yes** if the sentence makes sense or could possibly be true. Color **no** if it does not make sense or could not be true.

1. Pam is sad. | yes | no |

2. Ask Sam. | yes | no |

3. The pan sat. | yes | no |

4. A hat can grab. | yes | no |

5. Dan tags Jan. | yes | no |

6. Al pats the sad cat. | yes | no |

7. Jan is mad at Ann. | yes | no |

8. A bag can wag. | yes | no |

9. The ham is glad. | yes | no |

10. A man naps in a pan. | yes | no |

Sight words: no is the / yes in

Name_____

Directions for the student: **Practice reading 39 short a words on this page.** Choose 2-3 colors. Read each sentence or phrase. Pick the best answer and color it.

1. It is in Dad's hand.	mad | map
2. It is damp.	had | rag
3. Al is it.	rag | sad
4. Ann pats it.	cat | tan
5. Bad and mad	lap | Sam
6. It is fast.	sat | cab
7. Sam's hat	cap | rat
8. Jan and Pam	pals | map
9. Can clap	lamp | hands
10. It had a flat.	van | jam

Sight word: is / it in

Name_____

Directions for the student: **Practice reading 28 short a words on this page.** Choose 2-3 colors. Color **yes** if the sentence makes sense or could possibly be true. Color **no** if it does not make sense or could not be true.

1. Fat rats clap. | yes | no

2. Al had a plan. | yes | no

3. An ant had a hat. | yes | no

4. The bad man ran fast. | yes | no

5. The van had gas in it. | yes | no

6. Ham is in the pan. | yes | no

7. The cat can nap. | yes | no

8. Bags wag. | yes | no

9. Ask the jam. | yes | no

10. The map is Dad's. | yes | no

Name_____

Directions for the student: **Practice reading 38 short a words on this page.** Choose 2-3 colors. Read each sentence or phrase. Pick the best answer and color it.

1. It naps in Ann's lap. | cat | mad |

2. Trap it. | pan | rat |

3. A rag can be it. | had | damp |

4. It had a flat. | van | gas |

5. Bad Al | jam | brat |

6. Dan's is in a cast. | hand | map |

7. A dad is it. | man | bat |

8. Sam's is black. | bad | cap |

9. Pam's cat is it. | fat | rag |

10. A can is in it. | bag | sad |

Name_____

Directions for the student: Color **yes** if the sentence makes sense or could possibly be true. Color **no** if it does not make sense or could not be true.

1. A hand is sad. | yes | no |

2. A damp map naps. | yes | no |

3. Sam can clap. | yes | no |

4. Pass the ants. | yes | no |

5. Dan had black pants. | yes | no |

Directions for the student: Read each sentence or phrase. Pick the best answer and color it.

6. I can grab it. | add | map |

7. Jan had it. | bag | ran |

8. Ann's is black. | brat | hat |

9. In Al's hand | rag | man |

10. Can clap | hands | rat |

Sight words: no is the / yes it in

Name_____

Directions for the student: **Practice reading 28 short e words on this page.** Choose 2-3 colors. Color **yes** if the sentence makes sense or could possibly be true. Color **no** if it does not make sense or could not be true.

1. Eggs yell at Meg. | yes | no |

2. Get to bed, Jeff. | yes | no |

3. Deb's pen is red. | yes | no |

4. A jet is in the nest. | yes | no |

5. Ted is next to Jen. | yes | no |

6. Get on the sled. | yes | no |

7. Ben met ten men. | yes | no |

8. A pet can beg. | yes | no |

9. Tell the bed to get rest. | yes | no |

10. A desk has a neck. | yes | no |

Sight words: no to is the has / in on

Name_____

Directions for the student: **Practice reading 36 short e words on this page.** Choose 2-3 colors. Read each sentence or phrase. Pick the best answer and color it.

1. Deb rests in it.

pen	bed

2. I help Ken to mend it.

vest	ten

3. Its egg is in a nest.

hen	jet

4. A pet can do it.

web	beg

5. Sad Meg

egg	wept

6. Ted and Deb do it.

wed	bell

7. The last

peck	end

8. Jen's is red.

dress	send

9. Ed and Jeff left it.

leg	mess

10. A cat is it.

peg	pet

　　Sight words: to is de / in it its

Name_____

Directions for the student: **Practice reading 33 short e words on this page.** Choose 2-3 colors. Color *yes* if the sentence makes sense or could possibly be true. Color *no* if it does not make sense or could not be true.

1. Tell the desk to rest. | yes | no

2. Bess had a red belt. | yes | no

3. Ben dents Ed's van. | yes | no

4. Ten men fed the nest. | yes | no

5. Deb did best on a test. | yes | no

6. Jess had ten pets. | yes | no

7. Ed lent Ned a tent. | yes | no

8. Jen sent Meg a leg. | yes | no

9. Jeff fell in a well. | yes | no

10. Ken yells at Ted. | yes | no

Sight words: no the to / did on in   **11**

Name_____

Directions for the student: **Practice reading 36 short e words on this page.** Choose 2-3 colors. Read each sentence or phrase. Pick the best answer and color it.

1. Ed's is red.	vest	tell
2. Hens do it.	jet	peck
3. An egg is in it.	beg	nest
4. He met Ben.	Ken	leg
5. Jen's is red.	pen	bet
6. Bess can do it.	bell	help
7. Jeff slept in it.	men	tent
8. Do it to a cat.	pet	bet
9. Ken, Ted, and Ben	hen	men
10. Ed sells it.	get	desk

Sight words: is do he to / it in

Name_____

Directions for the student: **Practice reading 30 short e words on this page.** Choose 2-3 colors. Color **yes** if the sentence makes sense or could possibly be true. Color **no** if it does not make sense or could not be true.

1. Ed went to bed to rest. | yes | no |

2. Tell Jeff if Ken wept. | yes | no |

3. Deb lent Jen a belt. | yes | no |

4. A bell can step. | yes | no |

5. Sell Ted next. | yes | no |

6. The red pen slept. | yes | no |

7. Ben can spell. | yes | no |

8. The dress fell. | yes | no |

9. A jet bled. | yes | no |

10. Meg gets Jess an egg. | yes | no |

Sight words: no to the / if   **13**

Name_____

Directions for the student: **Practice reading 40 short e words on this page.** Choose 2-3 colors. Read each sentence or phrase. Pick the best answer and color it.

1. Deb mends it.

dress	bless

2. Jess, in a bed

slept	swept

3. Ed's bled.

nest	leg

4. Ken lent it to Jeff.

hen	sled

5. Bess had ten.

bells	fed

6. Jen's dress had it.

belt	stem

7. Pets do it.

beg	wed

8. Meg gets it.

yell	help

9. Naps help Jeff do it.

rest	egg

10. Ben fed it.

hen	red

14   Sight words: to do / it in

Name_____

Directions for the student: Color **yes** if the sentence makes sense or could possibly be true. Color **no** if it does not make sense or could not be true.

1. Ken's leg slept.

yes	no

2. Ed sells bent eggs.

yes	no

3. Deb begs Meg to tell.

yes	no

4. Jeff left a mess.

yes	no

5. Hens wed.

yes	no

Directions for the student: Read each sentence or phrase. Pick the best answer and color it.

6. Ted lent it to Ben.

peck	pen

7. It can bend.

leg	bell

8. Jen set it on a desk.

belt	end

9. Rest in it.

wed	bed

10. Get in it.

jet	best

Sight words: no to / it in on

Name_____

Directions for the student: **Practice reading 37 short i words on this page.** Choose 2-3 colors. Color **yes** if the sentence makes sense or could possibly be true. Color **no** if it does not make sense or could not be true.

1. Wigs hit and kick Kim.

yes	no

2. A bib fits Jim's dad.

yes	no

3. A pin can fix a rib.

yes	no

4. Sid hid his pill.

yes	no

5. Jill and Bill are six.

yes	no

6. Dip a rib in milk.

yes	no

7. Nick hid in the pig.

yes	no

8. Tim and Jim are twins.

yes	no

9. Bill bit his lip.

yes	no

10. Liz will win a big trip.

yes	no

Sight words: no his are

Name_____

Directions for the student: **Practice reading 54 short i words on this page.** Choose 2-3 colors. Read each sentence or phrase. Pick the best answer and color it.

1. Can kiss	pin	lips
2. Sid hid it.	rib	mitt
3. Tim will sit on it.	hill	bit
4. A pig is it.	big	dig
5. Jim did it to Bill.	mix	hit
6. Bill did it to Jim.	kick	sip
7. Kim will fix it.	dill	rip
8. Jill will sip it.	pill	milk
9. Liz will miss him.	fit	Rick
10. It can pick the skin.	pin	fill

Sight words: is to the / on

Name_____

Directions for the student: **Practice reading 37short i words on this page.** Choose 2-3 colors. Color **yes** if the sentence makes sense or could possibly be true. Color **no** if it does not make sense or could not be true.

1. A pig will fix Tim's lip. | yes | no |

2. Jill did a flip. | yes | no |

3. A kid is in the crib. | yes | no |

4. Pin the hill. | yes | no |

5. Six lips kick him. | yes | no |

6. A hip sips milk. | yes | no |

7. Kim wins a big trip. | yes | no |

8. Wigs kill pigs. | yes | no |

9. Bill fits in a pill. | yes | no |

10. Jim did rip his bib. | yes | no |

Sight words: no is the his   **19**

Name_____

Directions for the student: **Practice reading 51 short i words on this page.** Choose 2-3 colors. Read each sentence or phrase. Pick the best answer and color it.

1. He is a kid.

fix	Bill

2. Rick will lick it.

mint	mitt

3. Kim bit it.

hill	pill

4. It did fit Jim.

mitt	dig

5. Sid and Bill will do it.

hip	swim

6. It will fit the big pan.

lid	rib

7. Jill has six.

hips	pins

8. It did drip.

trip	milk

9. He will win.

lick	Rick

10. Tim and Liz do it.

kiss	bib

20   Sight words: he is do the has

Name_____

Directions for the student: **Practice reading 31 short i words on this page.** Choose 2-3 colors. Color *yes* if the sentence makes sense or could possibly be true. Color *no* if it does not make sense or could not be true.

1. A kid hit Liz. | yes | no |

2. Pigs kiss. | yes | no |

3. Jill will fix a rip. | yes | no |

4. The lid did fit the pan. | yes | no |

5. Jim bit a big brick. | yes | no |

6. A big kid will win. | yes | no |

7. Tim did swim. | yes | no |

8. Kill the wig. | yes | no |

9. The pin bit him. | yes | no |

10. Add milk and mix it. | yes | no |

Sight words: no the

Name_____

Directions for the student: **Practice reading 48 short i words on this page.** Choose 2-3 colors. Read each sentence or phrase. Pick the best answer and color it.

1. Tim will fix it.		drip	fin
2. Sick Bill had it.		pill	swim
3. Lips do it.		hip	kiss
4. Jill had it on.		wig	bit
5. Do it to milk.		pin	sip
6. Jim will do it.		lip	win
7. A kid will drip on it.		bib	hill
8. It is not big.		pin	miss
9. Rick will do it.		pig	trip
10. Liz had six.		mints	fix

Sight words: do to is / on not

Name_____

Directions for the student: Color **yes** if the sentence makes sense or could possibly be true. Color **no** if it does not make sense or could not be true.

1. Bill will win a lip. | yes | no |

2. I miss Rick's skin. | yes | no |

3. Swim in spit. | yes | no |

4. Pick Tim. | yes | no |

5. Kill the mint. | yes | no |

Directions for the student: Read each sentence or phrase. Pick the best answer and color it.

6. It is in Jim. | pin | rib |

7. Trip on it. | stick | sip |

8. Sid did drip on it. | bib | fill |

9. Lift it. | fit | brick |

10. The twins did it. | six | hid |

Sight words: no the is / on   **23**

Name_____

Directions for the student: **Practice reading 33 short o words on this page.** Choose 2-3 colors. Color **yes** if the sentence makes sense or could possibly be true. Color **no** if it does not make sense or could not be true.

1. Todd robs the fog. | yes | no |

2. Mom's pot is hot. | yes | no |

3. Don's cot is soft. | yes | no |

4. Ron's job is a cop. | yes | no |

5. Lock a dog in a pond. | yes | no |

6. A frog got off the rock. | yes | no |

7. Tom drops off the box. | yes | no |

8. Mom mops a lot. | yes | no |

9. Dolls hop on hogs. | yes | no |

10. Jon lost a sock. | yes | no |

Sight words: no the is   **25**

Name_____

Directions for the student: **Practice reading 38 short o words on this page.** Choose 2-3 colors. Read each sentence or phrase. Pick the best answer and color it.

1.	He stops Ron.	jog	cop
2.	A frog hops in it.	hog	pond
3.	It got lost.	doll	hot
4.	Stop! It's hot!	log	pot
5.	It is soft.	sock	rock
6.	Mom has it.	cop	mop
7.	Not on	god	off
8.	On Tom's dog	job	spot
9.	It cannot hop.	rock	frog
10.	Tick-tock	dog	clock

Sight words: he is has

Name_____

Directions for the student: **Practice reading 28 short o words on this page.** Choose 2-3 colors. Color **yes** if the sentence makes sense or could possibly be true. Color **no** if it does not make sense or could not be true.

1. Ron had on soft socks. | yes | no |

2. Todd's dog got lost. | yes | no |

3. A mop is hot. | yes | no |

4. Tom robs hogs. | yes | no |

5. Bob is Ron's boss. | yes | no |

6. A log is soft. | yes | no |

7. Fog is in the box. | yes | no |

8. Jon lost his job. | yes | no |

9. A cop stops Don. | yes | no |

10. Mom is a frog. | yes | no |

Sight words: no is his

Name_____

Directions for the student: **Practice reading 39 short o words on this page.** Choose 2-3 colors. Read each sentence or phrase. Pick the best answer and color it.

1. Can be in a box

| rocks | pond |

2. Sad Bob will do it.

| hog | sob |

3. Jon drops it.

| hop | box |

4. Ron's cot

| soft | fog |

5. Do not do it.

| fox | rob |

6. On a log at a pond

| frog | job |

7. He got lost.

| God | Ron |

8. Don's job

| cop | pot |

9. On Tom's socks

| hot | dots |

10. Todd will not do it.

| job | lost |

Sight words: be do he

Name_____

Directions for the student: **Practice reading 26 short o words on this page.** Choose 2-3 colors. Color *yes* if the sentence makes sense or could possibly be true. Color *no* if it does not make sense or could not be true.

1. Dolls hop. | yes | no |

2. Rocks rot. | yes | no |

3. Bob's dog has spots. | yes | no |

4. A frog has on socks. | yes | no |

5. Lock God in a box. | yes | no |

6. Tom is in the pond. | yes | no |

7. It cost a lot. | yes | no |

8. Ron is off his job. | yes | no |

9. Jon robs Don. | yes | no |

10. Cops toss mops. | yes | no |

Sight words: no has is the his

Name_____

Directions for the student: **Practice reading 36 short o words on this page.** Choose 2-3 colors. Read each sentence or phrase. Pick the best answer and color it.

1. Ron can toss it.

pond	rock

2. Don did it.

job	cob

3. Tom lost it.

not	sock

4. Bob naps on it.

cot	fox

5. Not off

hot	on

6. A cop did not do it.

cob	rob

7. A sock is in it.

hop	box

8. A pig

hog	rot

9. Mom's job to do

mop	top

10. A frog is on it.

hop	log

Sight words: do is to

Name_____

Directions for the student: Color **yes** if the sentence makes sense or could possibly be true. Color **no** if it does not make sense or could not be true.

1. A doll robs Tom.	yes | no
2. A fox will boss the dog.	yes | no
3. The cop stops Jon.	yes | no
4. Bob lost the lock.	yes | no
5. Don got hot.	yes | no

Directions for the student: Read each sentence or phrase. Pick the best answer and color it.

6. Not in a box	sock | fog
7. Soft	cot | rock
8. Ron's ran off.	dog | pot
9. Mom drops it.	hot | mop
10. It can stop.	clock | lot

Sight words: no the   **31**

Name_____

Directions for the student: **Practice reading 26 short u words on this page.** Choose 2-3 colors. Color **yes** if the sentence makes sense or could possibly be true. Color **no** if it does not make sense or could not be true.

1. Russ can hug a bug.　　| yes | no |

2. A mug can hum.　　| yes | no |

3. Rugs run and jump.　　| yes | no |

4. Gum is for a bus.　　| yes | no |

5. The sun is up.　　| yes | no |

6. The pup dug it up.　　| yes | no |

7. Just cut up the dust.　　| yes | no |

8. Gus cut the bun.　　| yes | no |

9. His gun had fun.　　| yes | no |

10. A bus can rust.　　| yes | no |

　　Sight words: no is for the his　　**33**

Name_____

Directions for the student: **Practice reading 34 short u words on this page.** Choose 2-3 colors. Read each sentence or phrase. Pick the best answer and color it.

1. I just dug in it.

mud	rug

2. It is up, up, up.

sub	sun

3. I must sit in it.

cub	bus

4. Fun for us to do

run	up

5. Russ will do it.

hum	bun

6. Gus bit it.

tug	nut

7. A cup

hug	mug

8. On a plum

gun	bug

9. For a tub

plug	cut

10. On a bus

must	rust

Sight words: is for to do

Name_____

Directions for the student: **Practice reading 26 short u words on this page.** Choose 2-3 colors. Color **yes** if the sentence makes sense or could possibly be true. Color **no** if it does not make sense or could not be true.

1. To Bud, it is fun to run. | yes | no |

2. Russ jumps on the sun. | yes | no |

3. A truck is stuck in mud. | yes | no |

4. It is bad luck to hum. | yes | no |

5. Just plug in the rug. | yes | no |

6. The tub had suds in it. | yes | no |

7. Gus hugs us. | yes | no |

8. The sun can buzz. | yes | no |

9. Guns tug on rugs. | yes | no |

10. Bugs rust. | yes | no |

Sight words: no is to the

Name_____

Directions for the student: **Practice reading 31 short u words on this page.** Choose 2-3 colors. Read each sentence or phrase. Pick the best answer and color it.

1. A truck is stuck in it.	mud	nut
2. Rust is on it.	dust	bus
3. I can do it.	cut	gun
4. Had to	rust	must
5. Do it to Dad.	hug	lump
6. It can buzz.	tug	bug
7. It can kill Russ.	drug	hug
8. A big cup	mug	luck
9. Just cut it up for us.	sun	bun
10. It is on a rug.	rub	mud

Sight words: is do to for

Name_____

Directions for the student: **Practice reading 29 short u words on this page.** Choose 2-3 colors. Color *yes* if the sentence makes sense or could possibly be true. Color *no* if it does not make sense or could not be true.

1. A bug dug up a tub. | yes | no |

2. Russ hugs the bus. | yes | no |

3. Ducks hum for fun. | yes | no |

4. A pup tugs at the rug. | yes | no |

5. The sun can run. | yes | no |

6. Guns buzz. | yes | no |

7. Gus cut up the mud. | yes | no |

8. Rub fuzz on cups. | yes | no |

9. Bud had gum for us. | yes | no |

10. Dad will tuck us in. | yes | no |

Sight words: no the for

Name_____

Directions for the student: **Practice reading 29 short u words on this page.** Choose 2-3 colors. Read each sentence or phrase. Pick the best answer and color it.

1. A pup did it.	jug	dug
2. It just bit Russ.	mug	bug
3. Bud is on it.	duck	bus
4. Pills	drugs	dust
5. Run and jump	nut	fun
6. Do it to a back	rug	rub
7. Bud hit it.	sun	drum
8. Gus bit it.	plum	gun
9. Sit in it.	tub	hug
10. A truck can do it.	lump	dump

Sight words: is do to for

Name_____

Directions for the student: Color **yes** if the sentence makes sense or could possibly be true. Color **no** if it does not make sense or could not be true.

1. The pup jumps up. | yes | no |

2. Dust the bug. | yes | no |

3. Gum can rust. | yes | no |

4. Russ hunts for us. | yes | no |

5. The rugs had fun. | yes | no |

Directions for the student: Read each sentence or phrase. Pick the best answer and color it.

6. A bump | tuck | lump |

7. It runs. | mug | bus |

8. In a tub | suds | sun |

9. On us | mud | just |

10. It can buzz. | plug | bug |

      Sight words: no the for   **39**

Name_____

Directions for the student: **Practice 24 a_e words on this page.** Choose 2-3 colors. Color *yes* if the sentence makes sense or could possibly be true. Color *no* if it does not make sense or could not be true.

1. James rakes the cake. | yes | no |

2. Apes save plates. | yes | no |

3. Dale can fix the brakes. | yes | no |

4. A cape is a cap. | yes | no |

5. Jane ate the cave. | yes | no |

6. Kids name gates. | yes | no |

7. Kate is late. | yes | no |

8. A grape can scare Abe. | yes | no |

9. Dave waves to Jane. | yes | no |

10. Wake the flakes. | yes | no |

Sight words: no the is to

Name_____

Directions for the student: **Practice reading 26 a_e words on this page.** Choose 2-3 colors. Read each sentence or phrase. Pick the best answer and color it.

1. Dave ate it.

plate	cake

2. Kate can go in it.

lake	ape

3. An old man has it.

cave	cane

4. It is wet.

wake	wave

5. It can go up.

plane	lake

6. It is a name.

fade	Jane

7. It is made of glass.

cake	vase

8. It can fix a rip.

tape	ate

9. It lets Nate in.

save	gate

10. Go get it for Dad.

rake	lake

Sight words: go old has is of for

Name_____

Directions for the student: **Practice reading 26 a_e words on this page.** Choose 2-3 colors. Color *yes* if the sentence makes sense or could possibly be true. Color *no* if it does not make sense or could not be true.

1. A cane is for a snake. | yes | no |

2. Dale and I trade games. | yes | no |

3. Nate gave Abe a lake. | yes | no |

4. Jake is late. | yes | no |

5. An ape has a mane. | yes | no |

6. "James" is a name. | yes | no |

7. Jane ate a plane. | yes | no |

8. Kids hate cake. | yes | no |

9. Kate wakes the tape. | yes | no |

10. Caves wave to Dave. | yes | no |

Sight words: no is for has the to

Name_____

Directions for the student: **Practice reading 27 a_e words on this page.** Choose 2-3 colors. Read each sentence or phrase. Pick the best answer and color it.

1. Dave swims in it.

take	lake

2. It is bad to do.

cake	hate

3. A hand can do it.

wake	wave

4. To get it and go

take	lake

5. Bats go in it.

plane	cave

6. Sells for less

sale	Dave

7. Kate made it.

wake	cake

8. Jane and Abe do it.

date	ape

9. Dale ate it.

grave	grape

10. Mom will do it.

bake	same

Sight words: is to do go for

Name_____

Directions for the student: **Practice reading 25 a_e words on this page.** Choose 2-3 colors. Color **yes** if the sentence makes sense or could possibly be true. Color **no** if it does not make sense or could not be true.

1. Wake Jake at six.

yes	no

2. James rakes the lake.

yes	no

3. Jane gave Dale a game.

yes	no

4. A plate can wave.

yes	no

5. A vase is for an ape.

yes	no

6. Snakes make gates.

yes	no

7. Save the cake for Dave.

yes	no

8. Kate takes a late nap.

yes	no

9. A jet is a plane.

yes	no

10. Tape the flame.

yes	no

Sight words: no the is for   **45**

Name_____

Directions for the student: **Practice reading 25 a_e words on this page.** Choose 2-3 colors. Read each sentence or phrase. Pick the best answer and color it.

1. Dave, Kate, Jane

names	gate

2. It is fun.

same	game

3. It can be red.

came	cape

4. Just skin

bare	cake

5. A fox can be in it.

cave	save

6. To step in a lake

wake	wade

7. It bit Dale.

snake	tape

8. Nap and get up.

wake	safe

9. "He did it, not me!"

blame	cape

10. It is hot.

flame	care

Sight words: is to do go for

Name_____

Directions for the student: Color **yes** if the sentence makes sense or could possibly be true. Color **no** if it does not make sense or could not be true.

1. Dave blames Dale.	yes	no
2. Wake the plate.	yes	no
3. Snakes rake.	yes	no
4. Jane tapes cakes.	yes	no
5. Abe ate grapes.	yes	no

Directions for the student: Read each sentence or phrase. Pick the best answer and color it.

6. It scares Kate.	same	snake
7. It is on sale.	game	flake
8. Stops a van	brake	cape
9. He is late.	trade	Jake
10. Get wet in it.	slave	lake

Sight words: no the is he   **47**

Name_____

Directions for the student: **Practice reading 19 ai words on this page.** Choose 2-3 colors. Color **yes** if the sentence makes sense or could possibly be true. Color **no** if it does not make sense or could not be true.

1. Gail paid the bill. | yes | no |

2. Snails fail tests. | yes | no |

3. Tim will nail his hair. | yes | no |

4. Trains sail on ponds. | yes | no |

5. A maid drains the tub. | yes | no |

6. Gail paints the air. | yes | no |

7. I mail rain. | yes | no |

8. Sand is in the pail. | yes | no |

9. A dog has a tail. | yes | no |

10. Send the pain to jail. | yes | no |

Sight words: no the his is has to

Name_____

Directions for the student: **Practice reading 23 ai words on this page.** Choose 2-3 colors. Read each sentence or phrase. Pick the best answer and color it.

1. Braid it.

pair	hair

2. Paint is in it.

tail	pail

3. On a cat

jail	tail

4. Clip it off.

nail	air

5. For bad men

sail	jail

6. A step

laid	stair

7. It will go on rails.

train	drain

8. It can be red.

paint	pain

9. A spot on a dress

stain	tail

10. Stop for a bit.

wait	paid

Sight words: is to do go for

Name_____

Directions for the student: **Practice reading 20 ai words on this page.** Choose 2-3 colors. Color **yes** if the sentence makes sense or could possibly be true. Color **no** if it does not make sense or could not be true.

1. He waits to get mail. | yes | no |

2. Paint can stain air. | yes | no |

3. A snail wags his tail. | yes | no |

4. I paint Gail's nails red. | yes | no |

5. Hair has pain. | yes | no |

6. A tail is in the pail. | yes | no |

7. Ed claims he paid bills. | yes | no |

8. Al trains dogs. | yes | no |

9. It rains in jail. | yes | no |

10. His waist is big. | yes | no |

Sight words: no he to his has is the

Name_____

Directions for the student: **Practice reading 21 ai words on this page.** Choose 2-3 colors. Read each sentence or phrase. Pick the best answer and color it.

1. It is in a can.

paint	pain

2. Dad hits it.

nail	rain

3. Send it.

mail	jail

4. Gail felt it.

pain	laid

5. A fan has it.

tail	air

6. Bad on a dress

stain	train

7. Step on it to go up.

stair	laid

8. A man has it.

tail	brain

9. 2

pair	tail

10. It can go fast.

train	hair

Sight words: is has to go

Name_____

Directions for the student: **Practice reading 21 ai words on this page.** Choose 2-3 colors. Color *yes* if the sentence makes sense or could possibly be true. Color *no* if it does not make sense or could not be true.

1. Red paint is in the pail.

yes	no

2. A train has a brain.

yes	no

3. Send the stair to jail.

yes	no

4. Dogs wait to get mail.

yes	no

5. Gail braids Mom's tail.

yes	no

6. Rain stains skin.

yes	no

7. Ed laid nails on a desk.

yes	no

8. Hair can faint.

yes	no

9. It will rain and hail.

yes	no

10. Drain air from the tub.

yes	no

Sight words: no is the has to   **53**

Name_____

Directions for the student: **Practice reading 21 ai words on this page.** Choose 2-3 colors. Read each sentence or phrase. Pick the best answer and color it.

1. Bad job on a test

rain	fail

2. I cut it.

air	hair

3. It is Gail's job.

pair	maid

4. It is wet.

rain	main

5. A belt is at it.

waist	rail

6. Did it to a bill

paid	fair

7. A dog wags it.

jail	tail

8. Sand is in it.

pail	mail

9. Run on it

tail	trail

10. Lock him in it.

jail	paid

Sight words: is to

Name_____

Directions for the student: Color **yes** if the sentence makes sense or could possibly be true. Color **no** if it does not make sense or could not be true.

1. I paid Gail for a brain. | yes | no |

2. Tails fail. | yes | no |

3. Trains faint. | yes | no |

4. He paints the stairs. | yes | no |

5. The maid has a pail. | yes | no |

Directions for the student: Read each sentence or phrase. Pick the best answer and color it.

6. A stamp is on it. | jail | mail |

7. Do it to hair. | nail | braid |

8. Can plug it | drain | waist |

9. Wait for it. | stain | train |

10. In a skull | brain | pair |

Sight words: no for he the has is

Name_____

Directions for the student: **Practice reading 23 ay words on this page.** Choose 2-3 colors. Color *yes* if the sentence makes sense or could possibly be true. Color *no* if it does not make sense or could not be true.

1. Cats pay bills. | yes | no |

2. Lay the clay on a tray. | yes | no |

3. Bugs pray on Sunday. | yes | no |

4. Ray had a bad day. | yes | no |

5. Jay can stay and play. | yes | no |

6. Dogs lay eggs. | yes | no |

7. Kay may say, "Okay." | yes | no |

8. Play clay can be gray. | yes | no |

9. Jay may lay it on a bed. | yes | no |

10. Hay is on the sun. | yes | no |

     Sight words: no the be is

Name_____

Directions for the student: **Practice reading 27 ay words on this page.** Choose 2-3 colors. Read each sentence or phrase. Pick the best answer and color it.

1. Ray plays with it.	say	clay

2. Say to God	pray	way

3. Set on a desk	lay	gray

4. Do not go.	tray	stay

5. Kay will do it to a bill.	pay	play

6. Hens can nest in it.	hay	bay

7. From the sun	ray	gray

8. Jay will do it.	hay	play

9. To tell it	stay	say

10. He may stay.	tray	Jay

Sight words: with to do go the

Name_____

Directions for the student: **Practice reading 21 ay words on this page.** Choose 2-3 colors. Color *yes* if the sentence makes sense or could possibly be true. Color *no* if it does not make sense or could not be true.

1. Gray cats pay for hay. | yes | no |

2. Tell Kay the way to go. | yes | no |

3. Jay bit the tray. | yes | no |

4. Kids play on the sun. | yes | no |

5. Ray may stay. | yes | no |

6. Kiss the clay and hay. | yes | no |

7. Dad lays eggs. | yes | no |

8. Dan plays in the hay. | yes | no |

9. Mom lays dust on trays. | yes | no |

10. I may pay him today. | yes | no |

Sight words: no for the to go

Name_____

Directions for the student: **Practice reading 27 ay words on this page.** Choose 2-3 colors. Read each sentence or phrase. Pick the best answer and color it.

1. Clay can be it.

| gray | way |

2. Say it to a dog.

| stay | hay |

3. Fun to do

| may | play |

4. A cup is on it.

| way | tray |

5. A man can do it.

| day | pray |

6. Hens do it to eggs.

| pay | lay |

7. He will stay away.

| Ray | hay |

8. For play

| clay | may |

9. Lips help Kay do it.

| tray | say |

10. Jay can jump in it.

| ray | hay |

Sight words: be to do is he for

Name_____

Directions for the student: **Practice reading 21 ay words on this page.** Choose 2-3 colors. Color **yes** if the sentence makes sense or could possibly be true. Color **no** if it does not make sense or could not be true.

1. Kay's clay is red. | yes | no

2. Jay may stay six days. | yes | no

3. It is okay to lay in a bed. | yes | no

4. Dad may say no. | yes | no

5. Cats lay gray eggs. | yes | no

6. Ray and Jay play tag. | yes | no

7. Pay the hay. | yes | no

8. His hat is gray. | yes | no

9. Kay got in the way. | yes | no

10. A tray can run. | yes | no

Sight words: no is to the

Name_____

Directions for the student: **Practice reading 26 ay words on this page.** Choose 2-3 colors. Read each sentence or phrase. Pick the best answer and color it.

1. A man	Jay | hay
2. May do it on Sunday	pray | way
3. The sun is up.	lay | day
4. Ray can lift it.	tray | play
5. Say if glad	yay | bay
6. A month	May | Ray
7. Fun to do	gray | play
8. May get Kay wet.	spray | pray
9. Yes	way | okay
10. A rock can be it.	day | gray

     Sight words: do is to be

Name_____

Directions for the student: Color yes if the sentence makes sense or could possibly be true. Color **yes** if the sentence makes sense or could possibly be true. Color **no** if it does not make sense or could not be true.

1. Do it Kay's way.

yes	no

2. The tray is gray.

yes	no

3. Ray may stay today.

yes	no

4. Play clay is for kids.

yes	no

5. The hay will say no.

yes	no

Directions for the student: Read each sentence or phrase. Pick the best answer and color it.

6. Ray's twin

say	Jay

7. It is wet.

spray	pay

8. Pick it up.

tray	day

9. Kay's pants

way	gray

10. To tell

may	say

Sight words: no do is the

Name_____

Directions for the student: **Practice reading 25 ee words on this page.** Choose 2-3 colors. Color *yes* if the sentence makes sense or could possibly be true. Color *no* if it does not make sense or could not be true.

1. We had beef last week. | yes | no |

2. Ed sees Al feed a deer. | yes | no |

3. A tree can peep. | yes | no |

4. I feel I need sleep. | yes | no |

5. Seeds can bleed. | yes | no |

6. Dee sleeps for a week. | yes | no |

7. A bee has big feet. | yes | no |

8. Lee meets Dee. | yes | no |

9. A queen can sneeze. | yes | no |

10. We need to feed feet. | yes | no |

Sight words: no we the for has to

Name_____

Directions for the student: **Practice reading 25 ee words on this page.** Choose 2-3 colors. Read each sentence or phrase. Pick the best answer and color it.

1. Dee plants it.

seed	peel

2. Sad Lee will do it.

peep	weep

3. It is green.

tree	meet

4. It can buzz.

feet	bee

5. Get the skin off.

peel	feed

6. See it on a street.

jeep	need

7. Men do not plant it.

tree	weed

8. No cost

deep	free

9. Can step and run

feed	feet

10. Must get

need	deep

Sight words: do is to be

Name_____

Directions for the student: **Practice reading 26 ee words on this page.** Choose 2-3 colors. Color *yes* if the sentence makes sense or could possibly be true. Color *no* if it does not make sense or could not be true.

1. Lee will keep the seeds. | yes | no |

2. Peel Dee's feet. | yes | no |

3. Dee seems sweet. | yes | no |

4. Feed teens trees. | yes | no |

5. See heels on feet. | yes | no |

6. I feel I will sneeze. | yes | no |

7. Bees weep and peep. | yes | no |

8. Get in Lee's jeep. | yes | no |

9. A weed can be green. | yes | no |

10. I need to get sleep. | yes | no |

Sight words: no the be to

Name_____

Directions for the student: **Practice reading 25 ee words on this page.** Choose 2-3 colors. Read each sentence or phrase. Pick the best answer and color it.

1. On feet

| heels | trees |

2. A nap

| weep | sleep |

3. Do not let it go.

| keep | see |

4. Dee meets him.

| need | Lee |

5. Get rid of it.

| weed | feed |

6. A nest is in it.

| jeep | tree |

7. At the end of legs

| bees | feet |

8. A hill can be it.

| seek | steep |

9. Not yet a man

| teen | seed |

10. Lee can feel it.

| breeze | peep |

68   Sight words: do go of the be

Name_____

Directions for the student: **Practice reading 23 ee words on this page.** Choose 2-3 colors. Color **yes** if the sentence makes sense or could possibly be true. Color **no** if it does not make sense or could not be true.

1. A seed has feet. | yes | no |

2. Lee is a teen. | yes | no |

3. Feed me a heel. | yes | no |

4. Eeeek! I see a bee! | yes | no |

5. Meet me next week. | yes | no |

6. Weeds beep. | yes | no |

7. Keep it for a week. | yes | no |

8. Dee sees a green jeep. | yes | no |

9. A tree peeks at him. | yes | no |

10. The teen went to sleep. | yes | no |

Sight words: no has is me for the to   **69**

Name_____

Directions for the student: **Practice reading 23 ee words on this page.** Choose 2-3 colors. Read each sentence or phrase. Pick the best answer and color it.

1. Dee will do it.

jeep	sweep

2. A nest is in it.

tree	peep

3. Lee will do it in bed.

sleep	tree

4. Had to get

feet	need

5. Grass is it.

peel	green

6. Sick Ben will do it.

teen	sneeze

7. Mom will fix it.

bee	beef

8. Lee's are big.

feet	free

9. Grab a lot

greed	see

10. A cut will do it.

bleed	need

Sight words: do is to are

Name_____

Directions for the student: Color **yes** if the sentence makes sense or could possibly be true. Color **no** if it does not make sense or could not be true.

1. Freeze the queen.

yes	no

2. Sweep the street.

yes	no

3. Dee needs to sneeze.

yes	no

4. Lee peels trees.

yes	no

5. Feel the breeze.

yes	no

Directions for the student: Read each sentence or phrase. Pick the best answer and color it.

6. Do it to a jeep.

steer	steep

7. Teens need it.

beer	sleep

8. It hid in the trees.

deer	beep

9. Need socks

feet	peep

10. It can bleed.

heel	weed

Sight words: no the to do

Name_____

Directions for the student: **Practice reading 25 long ea words on this page.** Choose 2-3 colors. Color *yes* if the sentence makes sense or could possibly be true. Color *no* if it does not make sense or could not be true.

1. A bean can leap. | yes | no

2. A mean kid is near Al. | yes | no

3. A seal has a beak. | yes | no

4. Ears can hear. | yes | no

5. Jean is clean and neat. | yes | no

6. We beat Dean's team. | yes | no

7. Meat has real tears. | yes | no

8. Please eat the peas. | yes | no

9. Neal reads at his seat. | yes | no

10. A dream can leak. | yes | no

Sight words: no has is we the his

Name_____

Directions for the student: **Practice reading 26 long ea words on this page.** Choose 2-3 colors. Read each sentence or phrase. Pick the best answer and color it.

1. Neal eats it.

seat	meat

2. Do it to a drum.

team	beat

3. It drips.

ear	leak

4. It is bad to be it.

neat	mean

5. From the sun

seal	heat

6. Jean hears me do it.

read	real

7. Sit on it.

seat	meat

8. Dean is on it.

fear	team

9. A cut will do it.

hear	heal

10. Dad heats it.

year	tea

Sight words: do to is be me

Name_____

Directions for the student: **Practice reading 22 long ea words on this page.** Choose 2-3 colors. Color *yes* if the sentence makes sense or could possibly be true. Color *no* if it does not make sense or could not be true.

1. Jean adds cream to tea. | yes | no |

2. His team beat us. | yes | no |

3. Clean up the grease. | yes | no |

4. Please be neat, Neal. | yes | no |

5. Dean is six years old. | yes | no |

6. A flea can speak. | yes | no |

7. Ears drip tears. | yes | no |

8. I sat near the fear. | yes | no |

9. A meal can leap. | yes | no |

10. Dad cleans his beak. | yes | no |

Sight words: no to his the be old   **75**

Name_____

Directions for the student: **Practice reading 28 long ea words on this page.** Choose 2-3 colors. Read each sentence or phrase. Pick the best answer and color it.

1. A duck has it.

beat	beak

2. Ears do it.

meat	hear

3. Heat and eat

beans	peaks

4. Pants

jeans	heat

5. Dean sips it.

gear	tea

6. Neal leans on it.

seat	fear

7. Sad Jean had it.

mean	tear

8. To get peas hot

leap	heat

9. Ham is it.

meat	year

10. It can swim.

lean	seal

Sight words: has do to is

Name_____

Directions for the student: **Practice reading 24 long ea words on this page.** Choose 2-3 colors. Color **yes** if the sentence makes sense or could possibly be true. Color **no** if it does not make sense or could not be true.

1. I can hear Neal's dream. | yes | no

2. Jean will clean the flea. | yes | no

3. A seat can speak. | yes | no

4. Neal beats on a drum. | yes | no

5. A seal sips tea. | yes | no

6. Dean will fix the leak. | yes | no

7. We will eat at the feast. | yes | no

8. Mom heats the peas. | yes | no

9. Seals steal jeans. | yes | no

10. At least eat the beans. | yes | no

Sight words: no the we

Name_____

Directions for the student: **Practice reading 28 long ea words on this page.** Choose 2-3 colors. Read each sentence or phrase. Pick the best answer and color it.

1. To hit and trip kids

bead	mean

2. Dean's do not fit.

east	jeans

3. It can hear.

beans	ear

4. It will win.

fear	team

5. In the back

rear	leap

6. Jean gets it.

treat	lean

7. To scrub

year	clean

8. Meat, beans, peas

leak	meal

9. Neal adds it to tea.

meat	cream

10. To yell

real	scream

Sight words: to do the

Name_____

Directions for the student: Color **yes** if the sentence makes sense or could possibly be true. Color **no** if it does not make sense or could not be true.

1. Jean heats the beans. | yes | no |

2. Cream can speak. | yes | no |

3. Neal eats dreams. | yes | no |

4. Dean's ears hear. | yes | no |

5. Grease his tears. | yes | no |

Directions for the student: Read each sentence or phrase. Pick the best answer and color it.

6. A dog had it. | flea | year |

7. On kids | beak | ear |

8. To jump | heat | leap |

9. Not a mess | neat | lean |

10. Near a desk | beat | seat |

     Sight words: no the his to   **79**

Name_____

Directions for the student: **Practice reading 23 vowel y / ey sounded /ē/ words on this page.** Choose 2-3 colors. Color *yes* if the sentence makes sense or could possibly be true. Color *no* if it does not make sense or could not be true.

1. Mickey will pass the jelly. | yes | no |

2. Kelly got on the trolley. | yes | no |

3. Jenny is a happy baby. | yes | no |

4. Billy feeds honey to rocks. | yes | no |

5. Joey has minty candy. | yes | no |

6. Pokey donkeys do flips. | yes | no |

7. A penny is crazy. | yes | no |

8. Candy can cost money. | yes | no |

9. The candy bag is empty. | yes | no |

10. Debby's monkey is funny. | yes | no |

Sight words: no the is has

Name_____

Directions for the student: **Practice reading 26 vowel y and ey words on this page.** Choose 2-3 colors. Read each sentence or phrase. Pick the best answer and color it.

1. Davey spends it.	lady | money
2. For a lock	valley | key
3. A belly	tummy | money
4. Hit the puck.	hockey | foggy
5. A tiny dog	sixty | puppy
6. Joey gets on its back.	donkey | penny
7. Sloppy	key | messy
8. Andy lost it.	money | bumpy
9. A cup can be it.	turkey | empty
10. Not fast	pokey | happy

Sight words: for the be

Name_____

Directions for the student: **Practice reading 23 vowel y and ey words on this page.** Choose 2-3 colors. Color **yes** if the sentence makes sense or could possibly be true. Color **no** if it does not make sense or could not be true.

1. Davey's kitty is tiny.

yes	no

2. Timmy bit the alley.

yes	no

3. Lindsey has fifty lips.

yes	no

4. Kelly sips the money.

yes	no

5. Hockey is for a pony.

yes	no

6. Honey is in chimneys.

yes	no

7. Tammy will copy Jimmy.

yes	no

8. Donkeys spend money.

yes	no

9. Randy had to study.

yes	no

10. Mickey's belly is empty.

yes	no

Sight words: no is the has for

Name_____

Directions for the student: **Practice reading 24 vowel y and ey words on this page.** Choose 2-3 colors. Read each sentence or phrase. Pick the best answer and color it.

1. Fun and fast

crabby	hockey

2. Bumpy land

hilly	pokey

3. Joey spills it.

honey	copy

4. An itty-bitty cat

donkey	kitty

5. It has legs.

turkey	ugly

6. She is not a man.

coney	lady

7. It jumps on a rock.

monkey	jelly

8. Wins a lot

chimney	lucky

9. It can get us in.

key	sloppy

10. Not sad

valley	happy

Sight words: has she

Name_____

Directions for the student: **Practice reading 23 vowel y and ey words on this page.** Choose 2-3 colors. Color *yes* if the sentence makes sense or could possibly be true. Color *no* if it does not make sense or could not be true.

1. Davey has fifty legs. | yes | no |

2. Monkeys sit in honey. | yes | no |

3. Jelly is waxy. | yes | no |

4. Billy pets the tiny kitty. | yes | no |

5. A lady spends money. | yes | no |

6. It is sunny and windy. | yes | no |

7. Joey's belly is empty. | yes | no |

8. Turkeys hug chimneys. | yes | no |

9. Zoey's tummy acts silly. | yes | no |

10. The puppy is in an alley. | yes | no |

    Sight words: no has is the

Name_____

Directions for the student: **Practice reading 30 vowel y and ey sounded /ē/ words on this page.** Choose 2-3 colors. Read each sentence or phrase. Pick the best answer and color it.

1. Wendy will do it.

study	money

2. Davey has ten.

keys	empty

3. Baby Joey is it.

fussy	turkey

4. Not sunny

foggy	hockey

5. The skinny kitty is it.

lazy	donkey

6. Timmy lost it.

penny	chimney

7. Kelly's desk

messy	valley

8. Not for kids

lucky	whiskey

9. A tummy

pokey	belly

10. A bus

alley	rusty

Sight words: do has is for

Name_____

Directions for the student: Color **yes** if the sentence makes sense or could possibly be true. Color **no** if it does not make sense or could not be true.

1. Billy will empty the box. | yes | no |

2. A turkey can copy. | yes | no |

3. A bunny spends money. | yes | no |

4. Jenny asks for the keys. | yes | no |

5. Joey has a lazy penny. | yes | no |

Directions for the student: Read each sentence or phrase. Pick the best answer and color it.

6. Not fat | honey | skinny |

7. Crabby | coney | grumpy |

8. Pet it. | puppy | money |

9. Sloppy | messy | pokey |

10. Mom stuffs it. | turkey | hilly |

     Sight words: no the for has

Name_____

Directions for the student: **Practice reading 24 i_e / ie words on this page.** Choose 2-3 colors. Color **yes** if the sentence makes sense or could possibly be true. Color **no** if it does not make sense or could not be true.

1. A kite can tell time.

yes	no

2. Al likes to bite tires.

yes	no

3. Kids ride bikes.

yes	no

4. Five and five is nine.

yes	no

5. Mike had a pile of dimes.

yes	no

6. Ike hides a dime.

yes	no

7. Wise men tell lies.

yes	no

8. Sam will hike a mile.

yes	no

9. Slime gets ripe.

yes	no

10. His wife is fine.

yes	no

Sight words: no to is of his

Name_____

Directions for the student: **Practice reading 22 i_e / ie words on this page.** Choose 2-3 colors. Read each sentence or phrase. Pick the best answer and color it.

1. Bad dogs do it.

bite	pipe

2. It is hot.

wide	fire

3. A plum can be it.

ripe	pine

4. Do it on a bike.

kite	ride

5. Dad has it on.

wide	tie

6. It went flat.

tire	ride

7. Mike did puff on it.

ripe	pipe

8. A box has it.

side	time

9. Mud is on it.

tile	fine

10. Yum!

pie	kite

Sight words: do is be has

Name_____

Directions for the student: **Practice reading 25 i_e / ie words on this page.** Choose 2-3 colors. Color **yes** if the sentence makes sense or could possibly be true. Color **no** if it does not make sense or could not be true.

1. A bike can smile. | yes | no |

2. Kids bite kites. | yes | no |

3. Mike tried nine times. | yes | no |

4. Ike can ride five miles. | yes | no |

5. It's fine to lie. | yes | no |

6. In time, plums get ripe. | yes | no |

7. Pipes can hike and hide. | yes | no |

8. Mike cut the wire. | yes | no |

9. The pie will die. | yes | no |

10. The dime is mine. | yes | no |

Sight words: no to do the is

Name_____

Directions for the student: **Practice reading 25 i_e / ie words on this page.** Choose 2-3 colors. Read each sentence or phrase. Pick the best answer and color it.

1. It is on a bike.

wine	tire

2. Do it to ham.

die	bite

3. Mom will wipe it.

tile	hire

4. Not for kids

bike	pipe

5. It will get Ed wet.

side	dive

6. It is for me.

mine	ripe

7. Mike can tell it.

time	tie

8. Dad likes to sip it.

wire	wine

9. It is in Al's hand.

wide	dime

10. Ride it.

pine	bike

Sight words: is to for me

Name_____

Directions for the student: **Practice reading 20 i_e / ie words on this page.** Choose 2-3 colors. Color *yes* if the sentence makes sense or could possibly be true. Color *no* if it does not make sense or could not be true.

1. Mike likes pie. | yes | no |

2. A wife can be ripe. | yes | no |

3. Wipe up the spill. | yes | no |

4. I can ride a dime. | yes | no |

5. A bike has five tires. | yes | no |

6. Fire is hot. | yes | no |

7. I like Dad's tie. | yes | no |

8. In time, plants die. | yes | no |

9. A kid has nine wives. | yes | no |

10. Ike fell off his bike. | yes | no |

Sight words: no be the has is   **93**

Name_____

Directions for the student: **Practice reading 25 i_e / ie words on this page.** Choose 2-3 colors. Read each sentence or phrase. Pick the best answer and color it.

1. Mike lost his.

ripe	bike

2. It can go up, up, up.

bite	kite

3. Bees can hide in it.

hire	hive

4. Ed likes to do it.

hike	side

5. I got a bite of it.

pie	dive

6. Time for a nap

tired	wire

7. A boss will do it.

wide	hire

8. A rag can do it.

wipe	smile

9. Ben won it.

hire	prize

10. Do not tell it.

lie	tie

Sight words: his go to do for

Name_____

Directions for the student: Color **yes** if the sentence makes sense or could possibly be true. Color **no** if it does not make sense or could not be true.

1. Hire Mike for the job.

yes	no

2. Dad has five ties.

yes	no

3. Ike likes to hike.

yes	no

4. Bite the fire.

yes	no

5. A dime ran a mile.

yes	no

Directions for the student: Read each sentence or phrase. Pick the best answer and color it.

6. 2 tires on it

kite	bike

7. To rob

time	crime

8. Lips do it

smile	rise

9. No life in him

die	ride

10. Dad will fix its drip.

smile	pipe

Sight words: no for the has to do   **95**

Name_____

Directions for the student: **Practice reading 16 igh words on this page.** Choose 2-3 colors. Color **yes** if the sentence makes sense or could possibly be true. Color **no** if it does not make sense or could not be true.

1. Dwight got in a fight. | yes | no |

2. A light can sigh. | yes | no |

3. He might be right. | yes | no |

4. A pig can jump high. | yes | no |

5. I had fright last night. | yes | no |

6. The sun is up at night. | yes | no |

7. The light is bright. | yes | no |

8. I will be right back. | yes | no |

9. He has on tight pants. | yes | no |

10. It is bright at night. | yes | no |

Sight words: no he be the is has   **97**

Name_____

Directions for the student: **Practice reading 22 igh words on this page.** Choose 2-3 colors. Read each sentence or phrase. Pick the best answer and color it.

1. Do not do it.

fight	tight

2. It is from the sun.

light	sigh

3. It is up, up, up.

might	high

4. Not left

night	right

5. A light can be it.

tight	bright

6. Dwight will do it.

sight	sigh

7. A vest on a fat man

flight	tight

8. Can I do it?

night	might

9. A scare

fright	sight

10. Not day

sigh	night

Sight words: do the be

Name_____

Directions for the student: **Practice reading 16 igh words on this page.** Choose 2-3 colors. Color **yes** if the sentence makes sense or could possibly be true. Color **no** if it does not make sense or could not be true.

1. The lid is on tight. | yes | no |

2. The men might fight. | yes | no |

3. The light will sigh. | yes | no |

4. Jan has a slight cut. | yes | no |

5. Sam might lick the light. | yes | no |

6. Dwight is a bright kid. | yes | no |

7. His sight might be bad. | yes | no |

8. Tuck me in at night. | yes | no |

9. The pill had a fright. | yes | no |

10. Tight pants might rip. | yes | no |

Name_____

Directions for the student: **Practice reading 22 igh words on this page.** Choose 2-3 colors. Read each sentence or phrase. Pick the best answer and color it.

1. I will be in bed.

sight	night

2. I got it from a mask.

fright	bright

3. The top step is it.

fight	high

4. A light can be it.

bright	might

5. His belt is it.

tight	sight

6. Sad Dan did it.

light	sigh

7. Yes, that's it.

fight	right

8. No light from the sun

tight	night

9. To hit and yell

right	fight

10. It is on, not off.

light	sigh

Sight words: do the be

Name_____

Directions for the student: **Practice reading 17 igh words on this page.** Choose 2-3 colors. Color **yes** if the sentence makes sense or could possibly be true. Color **no** if it does not make sense or could not be true.

1. Gus might get in a fight. | yes | no |

2. Dwight sighs. | yes | no |

3. Go right at the light. | yes | no |

4. Pigs fight cats. | yes | no |

5. The sun is up high. | yes | no |

6. Mud is bright. | yes | no |

7. Bugs fight at night. | yes | no |

8. That light is bright. | yes | no |

9. Ed might go right to bed. | yes | no |

10. The jet is high in flight. | yes | no |

Sight words: no the is go to   **101**

Name_____

Directions for the student: **Practice reading 22 igh words on this page.** Choose 2-3 colors. Read each sentence or phrase. Pick the best answer and color it.

1. The sun is it. | bright | tight |

2. Up on a shelf | high | sigh |

3. A lid can be it. | flight | tight |

4. Ed and Al might do it. | fight | night |

5. Shut it off. | might | light |

6. Do it if sad. | right | sigh |

7. On Jill's legs | tights | sight |

8. Not much | slight | high |

9. No sun | night | fight |

10. Glasses might help it. | fright | sight |

Sight words: the is be do

Name_____

Directions for the student: Color **yes** if the sentence makes sense or could possibly be true. Color **no** if it does not make sense or could not be true.

1. The light is up high. | yes | no |

2. A box might sigh. | yes | no |

3. She has fright at night. | yes | no |

4. Dwight's vest is tight. | yes | no |

5. The bright light is on. | yes | no |

Directions for the student: Read each sentence or phrase. Pick the best answer and color it.

6. Just a bit | sight | slight |

7. Bad to do | flight | fight |

8. A lamp | light | tight |

9. Not left | right | sigh |

10. If I can | bright | might |

     Sight words: no the is has to do

Name_____

Directions for the student: **Practice reading 21 vowel y sounded /ī/ words on this page.** Choose 2-3 colors. Color *yes* if the sentence makes sense or could possibly be true. Color *no* if it does not make sense or could not be true.

	yes	no
1. Mom will fry my box.	yes	no
2. Try to pry the lid.	yes	no
3. Step on the sky.	yes	no
4. My dog will try to fly.	yes	no
5. A fly can fly by us.	yes	no
6. A guy will buy my van.	yes	no
7. I will spy on him.	yes	no
8. A fly will cry.	yes	no
9. I will dry the sky.	yes	no
10. I dye my ribs red.	yes	no

Sight words: no to the

Name_____

Directions for the student: **Practice reading 20 vowel y sounded /ī/ words on this page.** Choose 2-3 colors. Read each sentence or phrase. Pick the best answer and color it.

1. A jet can do it.	cry | fly
2. The sun is in it.	sky | spy
3. Do it to wet hands.	fry | dry
4. Ask it.	sky | why
5. Can do it to ham.	fry | my
6. Do it if sad.	fly | cry
7. To go get it	fry | buy
8. A man	guy | try
9. Can do it to the lid.	spy | pry
10. It is a bug.	by | fly

Sight words: the is do to go

Name_____

Directions for the student: **Practice reading 17 vowel y sounded /ī/ words on this page.** Choose 2-3 colors. Color **yes** if the sentence makes sense or could possibly be true. Color **no** if it does not make sense or could not be true.

	yes	no
1. Dry the fry pan.	yes	no
2. Bugs spy on us.	yes	no
3. Try to do a bad job.	yes	no
4. The fly will cry.	yes	no
5. Dye the rug red.	yes	no
6. I will dry my hand.	yes	no
7. Jets fly in the sky.	yes	no
8. Sit by my desk.	yes	no
9. That guy is a spy.	yes	no
10. Buy Dad the sky.	yes	no

Sight words: the to do that is

Name_____

Directions for the student: **Practice reading 22 vowel y sounded /ī/ words on this page.** Choose 2-3 colors. Read each sentence or phrase. Pick the best answer and color it.

1. Dad will kill it.	fry	fly
2. Do it to get a lid up.	fly	pry
3. A jet will fly in it.	sky	spy
4. Do it in a pan.	cry	fry
5. That sad guy will do it.	my	cry
6. A kid can do it.	try	sky
7. It got on the ham.	sky	fly
8. Next to	by	cry
9. Not wet	spy	dry
10. Ron is it.	guy	fly

Sight words: that do to the is

Name_____

Directions for the student: **Practice reading 17 vowel y sounded /ī/ words on this page.** Choose 2-3 colors. Color **yes** if the sentence makes sense or could possibly be true. Color **no** if it does not make sense or could not be true.

1. Fry the sky.	yes	no
2. The spy got mad.	yes	no
3. Ryan asks why.	yes	no
4. My dad will try.	yes	no
5. A pig can fly.	yes	no
6. A wet pond is dry.	yes	no
7. Mom will fry a fly.	yes	no
8. A guy will buy the sky.	yes	no
9. Tell me why he did it.	yes	no
10. My mom will fry eggs.	yes	no

Sight words: no the is me he

Name_____

Directions for the student: **Practice reading 25 vowel y sounded /ī/ words on this page.** Choose 2-3 colors. Read each sentence or phrase. Pick the best answer and color it.

1. A rag can do it.	dry	by
2. Ed, Al, and Tom	guys	pry
3. I will do my best.	dry	try
4. It will fly in the sky.	my	fly
5. Sad kids do it.	cry	fry
6. Can get cloth red.	my	dye
7. To hide and see	sky	spy
8. It is up by the sun.	dry	sky
9. Do it to ham.	fry	cry
10. He hides by mom.	shy	buy

Sight words: do to the is

Name_____

Directions for the student: Color **yes** if the sentence makes sense or could possibly be true. Color **no** if it does not make sense or could not be true.

1. A fly buys gum. | yes | no |

2. Ask why he did it. | yes | no |

3. Spy on the bad guy. | yes | no |

4. Dye the sky red. | yes | no |

5. Go sit by Guy. | yes | no |

Directions for the student: Read each sentence or phrase. Pick the best answer and color it.

6. Spend to get | why | buy |

7. See if I can do it. | try | sky |

8. To get the wet off | fly | dry |

9. See it up by the sun. | cry | sky |

10. I met him. | guy | fry |

     Sight words: no he the go to do

Name_____

Directions for the student: **Practice reading 19 o_e / oe words on this page.** Choose 2-3 colors. Color **yes** if the sentence makes sense or could possibly be true. Color **no** if it does not make sense or could not be true.

1. Rose will go home.　　　　| yes | no |

2. His toe is sore.　　　　| yes | no |

3. The mole dug a hole.　　　　| yes | no |

4. I wore a robe.　　　　| yes | no |

5. A pole can hope.　　　　| yes | no |

6. Joe woke the rose.　　　　| yes | no |

7. The joke went home.　　　　| yes | no |

8. Kids smoke.　　　　| yes | no |

9. The dog had a bone.　　　　| yes | no |

10. Joel dove in the pond.　　　　| yes | no |

　　Sight words: no go his is the

Name_____

Directions for the student: **Practice reading 23 o_e / oe words on this page.** Choose 2-3 colors. Read each sentence or phrase. Pick the best answer and color it.

1. It can smell a rose.

hole	nose

2. I fell and broke it.

poke	bone

3. Joe will tell it.

joke	mole

4. A stick can do it.

poke	lone

5. Dig it.

zone	hole

6. Up from a nap

woke	toe

7. A flag is on its top.

tone	pole

8. Jump it

rope	role

9. It can be red.

more	rose

10. A cut can be it.

sore	rode

Sight words: do is be

Name_____

Directions for the student: **Practice reading 21 o_e / oe words on this page.** Choose 2-3 colors. Color **yes** if the sentence makes sense or could possibly be true. Color **no** if it does not make sense or could not be true.

1. Joe picks a rose. | yes | no |

2. Sam woke up. | yes | no |

3. I hope my toe froze. | yes | no |

4. Joel got more votes. | yes | no |

5. A flag pole tells jokes. | yes | no |

6. Ed's nose smells smoke. | yes | no |

7. I woke the stone. | yes | no |

8. Rose tore up the note. | yes | no |

9. Dan broke a bone. | yes | no |

10. A robe is for a bug. | yes | no |

Sight words: no the is for

Name_____

Directions for the student: **Practice reading 24 o_e / oe words on this page.** Choose 2-3 colors. Read each sentence or phrase. Pick the best answer and color it.

1. A dog bit it.

joke	bone

2. Smell it.

hole	rose

3. A rock

stone	robe

4. A man

toe	Joe

5. Dan broke it.

bone	home

6. Dad dug it.

hole	woke

7. Joel did tell it.

dove	joke

8. It is sore.

toe	hope

9. Tug on it.

rope	lone

10. It can smell smoke.

nose	woke

Sight words: is

Name_____

Directions for the student: **Practice reading 21 o_e / oe words on this page.** Choose 2-3 colors. Color *yes* if the sentence makes sense or could possibly be true. Color *no* if it does not make sense or could not be true.

1. I will vote for Rose. | yes | no |

2. Mom drove Joel home. | yes | no |

3. I tore the stone. | yes | no |

4. Tell more jokes. | yes | no |

5. Joe has a sore nose. | yes | no |

6. I woke the bone. | yes | no |

7. A hole is in his robe. | yes | no |

8. A stove has toes. | yes | no |

9. The rose hid a note. | yes | no |

10. I got a jump rope. | yes | no |

     Sight words: no for the has is his

Name_____

Directions for the student: **Practice reading 26 o_e / oe words on this page.** Choose 2-3 colors. Read each sentence or phrase. Pick the best answer and color it.

1. Do not pick it.

nose	woke

2. Joe did it to his van.

stone	drove

3. Mom's broke.

stove	joke

4. A dog's bone is in it.

mole	hole

5. Joel has ten.

broke	toes

6. Ann sniffs it.

hole	rose

7. It is fun to tell.

joke	woke

8. Jen wore it.

toe	robe

9. Glass did it.

rope	broke

10. I tore it up.

nose	note

Sight words: do to his is has

Check-up Long o_e and **oe** (as in j**o**k**e** and t**oe**)

Name_____

Directions for the student: Color **yes** if the sentence makes sense or could possibly be true. Color **no** if it does not make sense or could not be true.

1. Ed woke up Rose.

yes	no

2. Ropes tell jokes.

yes	no

3. Dad drove Joe home.

yes	no

4. Toes snore.

yes	no

5. I rode the stove.

yes	no

Directions for the student: Read each sentence or phrase. Pick the best answer and color it.

6. In holes dogs dig

woke	bones

7. Did rip it

role	tore

8. Smell it.

lone	smoke

9. Dad wore it.

robe	vote

10. Mom will go to it.

store	froze

Sight words: no the go to   **119**

Name_____

Directions for the student: **Practice reading 17 oa words on this page.** Choose 2-3 colors. Color **yes** if the sentence makes sense or could possibly be true. Color **no** if it does not make sense or could not be true.

1. Al can toast a road.	yes	no
2. Goats float on foam.	yes	no
3. His goal is to win.	yes	no
4. Soap is red.	yes	no
5. Coal moans.	yes	no
6. A boat can float.	yes	no
7. Soak the rag.	yes	no
8. Ed will roast hot dogs.	yes	no
9. Joan got in the boat.	yes	no
10. His coat fits a goat.	yes	no

Sight words: no his is to the   **121**

Name_____

Directions for the student: **Practice reading 21 oa words on this page.** Choose 2-3 colors. Read each sentence or phrase. Pick the best answer and color it.

1. It has a crust.

toast	boat

2. To get wet

soak	croak

3. Gets mud off

coal	soap

4. To brag

boast	loan

5. Toads do it.

load	croak

6. It has legs.

soak	goat

7. A van is on it.

float	road

8. It can be red.

moan	coat

9. It hops.

goal	toad

10. To lend

oak	loan

Sight words: has to do is be

Name_____

Directions for the student: **Practice reading 18 oa words on this page.** Choose 2-3 colors. Color *yes* if the sentence makes sense or could possibly be true. Color *no* if it does not make sense or could not be true.

1. Soap is for toast.	yes	no
2. Roads croak.	yes	no
3. Dan has a red coat.	yes	no
4. Mom will roast a toad.	yes	no
5. I will soak in the tub.	yes	no
6. Load coal on the truck.	yes	no
7. A goat can roar.	yes	no
8. His coat got wet.	yes	no
9. Joan moans and groans.	yes	no
10. Boats float.	yes	no

Sight words: no is for has the his

Name_____

Directions for the student: **Practice reading 24 oa words on this page.** Choose 2-3 colors. Read each sentence or phrase. Pick the best answer and color it.

1. To fill up a truck	load	oak
2. It will float.	goat	boat
3. It is black.	coal	soak
4. A bus will go on it.	soap	road
5. "I am the best!"	boast	load
6. It bit Joan.	coat	goat
7. A toad will not do it.	roar	croak
8. Zip it.	goat	coat
9. I had it in the tub.	soap	coal
10. Joan had jam on it.	soak	toast

Sight words: to is go the do

Name_____

Directions for the student: **Practice reading 19 oa words on this page.** Choose 2-3 colors. Color **yes** if the sentence makes sense or could possibly be true. Color **no** if it does not make sense or could not be true.

1. Loan Joan a coat. | yes | no |

2. Toads kiss goats. | yes | no |

3. The road roars. | yes | no |

4. Soap moans. | yes | no |

5. Al will roast the boat. | yes | no |

6. To boast is to brag. | yes | no |

7. Toast is made of foam. | yes | no |

8. The goat ate the oats. | yes | no |

9. Coals can be hot. | yes | no |

10. Coats fit toads. | yes | no |

Sight words: no the to is of be   **125**

Name_____

Directions for the student: **Practice reading 23 oa words on this page.** Choose 2-3 colors. Read each sentence or phrase. Pick the best answer and color it.

1. We can cross it.

road	coal

2. Can get a boat to go.

roar	oars

3. To brag

boast	roast

4. Tim's is black.

loan	coat

5. A boat can do it.

soap	float

6. It has legs.

goat	moan

7. Can do it to a rag.

croak	soak

8. Suds it up.

toast	soap

9. Joan had them.

oats	foam

10. A neck

throat	boat

Sight words: we to go is do has

Name_____

Directions for the student: Color **yes** if the sentence makes sense or could possibly be true. Color **no** if it does not make sense or could not be true.

1. Toast the boat. | yes | no |

2. Coats croak. | yes | no |

3. Roads float. | yes | no |

4. Joan will fix a roast. | yes | no |

5. Goats lick foam. | yes | no |

Directions for the student: Read each sentence or phrase. Pick the best answer and color it.

6. In the tub | load | soap |

7. Jam is on it. | road | toast |

8. Sit in it. | roar | boat |

9. Can get hot. | coals | foam |

10. Joan had it on. | boast | coat |

Sight words: no the is   **127**

Name_____

Directions for the student: **Practice reading 15 long ow words on this page.** Choose 2-3 colors. Color *yes* if the sentence makes sense or could possibly be true. Color *no* if it does not make sense or could not be true.

	yes	no
1. Ron has a yellow bowl.	yes	no
2. I grow a row of ants.	yes	no
3. Crows glow.	yes	no
4. Dad mows the grass.	yes	no
5. Blow up the sun.	yes	no
6. Ann's elbow is slow.	yes	no
7. Dan owns a tow truck.	yes	no
8. The dress has a bow.	yes	no
9. Snow is hot.	yes	no
10. A rug will grow.	yes	no

Sight words: no of the is has

Name_____

Directions for the student: **Practice reading 21 long ow words on this page.** Choose 2-3 colors. Read each sentence or phrase. Pick the best answer and color it.

1. Do it to grass.

tow	mow

2. Mom owns it.

bowl	slow

3. Kids do it.

snow	grow

4. Lips do it.

blow	bowl

5. Not up

low	glow

6. It is black.

crow	flow

7. Nuts can be in it.

tow	bowl

8. It is cold.

snow	mow

9. A truck can do it.

tow	grow

10. Not fast

row	slow

Sight words: do to is be

Name_____

Directions for the student: **Practice reading 16 long ow words on this page.** Choose 2-3 colors. Color *yes* if the sentence makes sense or could possibly be true. Color *no* if it does not make sense or could not be true.

1. Tim mows snow.

yes	no

2. Set the bowls in a row.

yes	no

3. A crow can grow.

yes	no

4. Ben owns a slow van.

yes	no

5. Send for a tow truck.

yes	no

6. The snow will grow up.

yes	no

7. Crows own dogs.

yes	no

8. Mom did drop a bowl.

yes	no

9. Sit on the low step.

yes	no

10. Pigs glow.

yes	no

Sight words: no the for

Name_____

Directions for the student: **Practice reading 21 long ow words on this page.** Choose 2-3 colors. Read each sentence or phrase. Pick the best answer and color it.

1. Brrrrrrr! | crow | snow |

2. The desks are in it. | row | bowl |

3. Ed can own it. | bowl | snow |

4. It is on Jan's dress. | glow | bow |

5. A truck can do it. | tow | row |

6. Wind will do it. | mow | blow |

7. It has a crack in it. | glow | bowl |

8. It is to get big. | grow | low |

9. Tracks can be in it. | flow | snow |

10. To cut the grass | crow | mow |

Sight words: are is do has to be the

Name_____

Directions for the student: **Practice reading 15 long ow words on this page.** Choose 2-3 colors. Color **yes** if the sentence makes sense or could possibly be true. Color **no** if it does not make sense or could not be true.

1. We mow rugs. | yes | no |

2. He owns a yellow van. | yes | no |

3. A jet is slow. | yes | no |

4. Elbows glow. | yes | no |

5. Crows are yellow. | yes | no |

6. I nap on a pillow. | yes | no |

7. Ann owns the bows. | yes | no |

8. A crow can blow. | yes | no |

9. Jam is in the bowl. | yes | no |

10. Tom will grow up. | yes | no |

    Sight words: no we he is are the

Name_____

Directions for the student: **Practice reading 21 long ow words on this page.** Choose 2-3 colors. Read each sentence or phrase. Pick the best answer and color it.

1. Mom and Dad do it.

crow	bowl

2. A tow truck can be it.

glow	yellow

3. It is in a nest.

crow	low

4. A man

grown	flow

5. A fan will do it.

snow	blow

6. It is mine.

own	glow

7. It bends.

slow	elbow

8. Kids jump in it.

bowl	snow

9. Plant seeds in it.

row	grow

10. It can be soft.

mow	pillow

Sight words: do be is

Name_____

Directions for the student: Color **yes** if the sentence makes sense or could possibly be true. Color **no** if it does not make sense or could not be true.

1. Bowls go slow. | yes | no |

2. He has a yellow pillow. | yes | no |

3. Snow glows. | yes | no |

4. Grown-ups will grow old. | yes | no |

5. A crow has bows. | yes | no |

Directions for the student: Read each sentence or phrase. Pick the best answer and color it.

6. Grass will do it. | flow | grow |

7. It can be yellow. | low | bow |

8. On a bed | pillow | crow |

9. Hit the pins | snow | bowl |

10. 2 on a man | glow | elbows |

Sight words: no he has old do be   **135**

Long u_e and **ue** (as in **tu**be, **use**, and bl**ue**)

Name_____

Directions for the student: **Practice reading 17 u_e / ue words on this page.** Choose 2-3 colors. Color *yes* if the sentence makes sense or could possibly be true. Color *no* if it does not make sense or could not be true.

1. Fuel can cure the sick. | yes | no |

2. Kiss the tube of glue. | yes | no |

3. A mule did kick Duke. | yes | no |

4. Luke can be rude. | yes | no |

5. Prunes hum tunes. | yes | no |

6. A cube can get fat. | yes | no |

7. The flute will kick me. | yes | no |

8. We will see him in June. | yes | no |

9. Use glue to stick it. | yes | no |

10. Sue is cute. | yes | no |

Sight words: no the of be to is

Name_____

Directions for the student: **Practice reading 22 u_e / ue words on this page.** Choose 2-3 colors. Read each sentence or phrase. Pick the best answer and color it.

1. It can be hot.	use	June

2. Luke hums it.	cure	tune

3. Sue's dress is it.	Duke	blue

4. It is for us to do.	rule	cube

5. It will fix the sick.	cure	June

6. It has a pit.	prune	flute

7. It has legs.	rude	mule

8. Dad's bill is it.	cube	due

9. In a tube	glue	mule

10. To bump and go on	rude	June

Sight words: be is for do the has to go

Name_____

Directions for the student: **Practice reading 16 u_e / ue words on this page.** Choose 2-3 colors. Color **yes** if the sentence makes sense or could possibly be true. Color **no** if it does not make sense or could not be true.

1. A mule can cure Dan. | yes | no |

2. It is cute to be rude. | yes | no |

3. Sue will kiss Luke. | yes | no |

4. We glue lips. | yes | no |

5. The bill is due in June. | yes | no |

6. Pigs hum tunes. | yes | no |

7. Use a blue pen. | yes | no |

8. His dog did puke. | yes | no |

9. It is true. | yes | no |

10. Duke can be cruel. | yes | no |

Sight words: no is to be we his

Name_____

Directions for the student: **Practice reading 21 u_e / ue words on this page.** Choose 2-3 colors. Read each sentence or phrase. Pick the best answer and color it.

1. It can kick.

mule	rule

2. Gas

fuel	cube

3. Smell them.

flutes	fumes

4. It sticks.

glue	rude

5. He cut in front of me.

rude	cure

6. We plan a trip in it.

June	Luke

7. A pill

cure	cube

8. He will go to bed.

glue	Duke

9. It is big, big, big!

huge	fuel

10. Luke's vest

due	blue

Sight words: of me we go to is

Name_____

Directions for the student: **Practice reading 18 u_e / ue words on this page.** Choose 2-3 colors. Color *yes* if the sentence makes sense or could possibly be true. Color *no* if it does not make sense or could not be true.

1. A cube can be rude.

yes	no

2. Mules spit fuel.

yes	no

3. Ed's cat is cute.

yes	no

4. It can be hot in June.

yes	no

5. Hens can hum tunes.

yes	no

6. Glue is in the blue tube.

yes	no

7. A pill can cure Duke.

yes	no

8. Luke is rude to flutes.

yes	no

9. Sue has a cute dress.

yes	no

10. A rule is "Do not run."

yes	no

Sight words: no be is the to has

Name_____

Directions for the student: **Practice reading 23 u_e / ue words on this page.** Choose 2-3 colors. Read each sentence or phrase. Pick the best answer and color it.

1. It is in Luke's van.

cute	fuel

2. It can fix stuff.

glue	mule

3. From a flute

tune	fumes

4. Not little

due	huge

5. A sick cat did do it.

puke	prune

6. Do not be rude.

rule	huge

7. It is on the flag.

fuel	blue

8. It has legs.

mule	tube

9. Can be a hot month.

Duke	June

10. Gas has them.

rude	fumes

Sight words: little do be has

Name_____

Directions for the student: Color **yes** if the sentence makes sense or could possibly be true. Color **no** if it does not make sense or could not be true.

1. Sue will use the glue. | yes | no |

2. The prune is cruel. | yes | no |

3. Luke will cure the tube. | yes | no |

4. It is true milk is blue. | yes | no |

5. A flute is for a mule. | yes | no |

Directions for the student: Read each sentence or phrase. Pick the best answer and color it.

6. A hint | tune | clue |

7. Pants can be it. | blue | fuse |

8. Duke bit it. | tube | prune |

9. Sue smells it. | fume | June |

10. Get on its back. | mule | flute |

Sight words: no the is for be   **143**

Name_____

Directions for the student: **Practice reading 12 ui words on this page.** Choose 2-3 colors. Color **yes** if the sentence makes sense or could possibly be true. Color **no** if it does not make sense or could not be true.

1. Dress fruit in a suit. | yes | no |

2. Sip the fruit juice. | yes | no |

3. Ed will bruise the pan. | yes | no |

4. Ann got a swim suit. | yes | no |

5. A ship can cruise. | yes | no |

6. Juice can be red. | yes | no |

7. Dan got a bad bruise. | yes | no |

8. Tom will ruin his test. | yes | no |

9. Dad had on a suit. | yes | no |

10. Cats pick fruit. | yes | no |

     Sight words: no the be his

Name_____

Directions for the student: **Practice reading 21 ui words on this page.** Choose 2-3 colors. Read each sentence or phrase. Pick the best answer and color it.

1. Pick it.

ruin	fruit

2. It is on skin.

bruise	ruin

3. A plum

fruit	cruise

4. Sip it.

suit	juice

5. Get it on for a swim.

bruise	suit

6. Get it from fruit.

juice	ruin

7. A ship will do it.

bruise	cruise

8. To mess it up

juice	ruin

9. I bit it.

fruit	cruise

10. It can be red.

ruin	suit

Sight words: is for do to be

Name_____

Directions for the student: **Practice reading 12 ui words on this page.** Choose 2-3 colors. Color *yes* if the sentence makes sense or could possibly be true. Color *no* if it does not make sense or could not be true.

1. Tim did ruin his suit.	yes | no
2. Ann had a big bruise!	yes | no
3. Plant fruit in ponds.	yes | no
4. Dress pigs in suits.	yes | no
5. Jen went on a cruise.	yes | no
6. Dad's suit fits a bug.	yes | no
7. Get fruit from hens.	yes | no
8. Hugs ruin kids.	yes | no
9. I got sick on a cruise.	yes | no
10. Juice can get a bruise.	yes | no

　　　　Sight words: no his　　　　**147**

Name_____

Directions for the student: **Practice reading 20 ui words on this page.** Choose 2-3 colors. Read each sentence or phrase. Pick the best answer and color it.

1. It will fit me.

suit	bruise

2. Mom cut it up.

juice	fruit

3. From when I got hit.

cruise	bruise

4. It is in a glass.

suit	juice

5. Dad got a spot on it.

juice	suit

6. If I rip the test

ruin	fruit

7. It can spill.

juice	cruise

8. Tim fell and got it.

bruise	juice

9. A snack

suit	fruit

10. I had it on to swim.

juice	suit

Sight words: me is the the to

Name_____

Directions for the student: **Practice reading 12 ui words on this page.** Choose 2-3 colors. Color *yes* if the sentence makes sense or could possibly be true. Color *no* if it does not make sense or could not be true.

1. Do not ruin the dress. | yes | no |

2. Juice is from fruit. | yes | no |

3. I had on a swim suit. | yes | no |

4. Bruise the sand. | yes | no |

5. Ben spills his juice. | yes | no |

6. Pin the fruit. | yes | no |

7. The suit fits the cat. | yes | no |

8. A cruise is for pigs. | yes | no |

9. Mud can ruin a suit. | yes | no |

10. Ham is a fruit. | yes | no |

Sight words: no do the is his for

Name_____

Directions for the student: **Practice reading 20 ui words on this page.** Choose 2-3 colors. Read each sentence or phrase. Pick the best answer and color it.

1. Dad's is big on me.

| suit | cruise |

2. From good to bad

| ruin | cruise |

3. It is from apples.

| suit | juice |

4. It is in Ann's lunch.

| cruise | fruit |

5. A stack of blocks fell

| juice | ruin |

6. On Ron's leg

| bruise | cruise |

7. Ted bit into it.

| juice | fruit |

8. Can do it on a trip.

| cruise | suit |

9. It is in a cup.

| ruin | juice |

10. Pants go with it.

| suit | fruit |

Sight words: is me good of into do go

Name_____

Directions for the student: Color **yes** if the sentence makes sense or could possibly be true. Color **no** if it does not make sense or could not be true.

1. The sun will bruise us.

yes	no

2. Cruise on a desk.

yes	no

3. Mom got fruit for me.

yes	no

4. He will bruise the juice.

yes	no

5. Pigs swim in suits.

yes	no

Directions for the student: Read each sentence or phrase. Pick the best answer and color it.

6. Snack on it.

fruit	ruin

7. It fits.

ruin	suit

8. Can be on a kid

bruise	fruit

9. End up in a mess

cruise	ruin

10. From fruit

juice	cruise

Sight words: no the for he be   **151**

Name_____

Directions for the student: **Practice reading 20 sh words on this page.** Choose 2-3 colors. Color **yes** if the sentence makes sense or could possibly be true. Color **no** if it does not make sense or could not be true.

1. Trish picks up the trash. | yes | no |

2. Flush the wish. | yes | no |

3. Shut the shed for Dad. | yes | no |

4. She got a shock. | yes | no |

5. The fish shot Sam. | yes | no |

6. Josh did smash a dish. | yes | no |

7. I will shop for a brush. | yes | no |

8. The dish had a rash. | yes | no |

9. The van did crash. | yes | no |

10. I wish I had cash. | yes | no |

Name_____

Directions for the student: **Practice reading 23 sh words on this page.** Choose 2-3 colors. Read each sentence or phrase. Pick the best answer and color it.

1. Josh locks it.

brush	shed

2. Trish went to do it.

ship	shop

3. She did it with a gun.

cash	shot

4. Ham is on it.

shut	dish

5. Go fast.

rush	ash

6. Red on skin

dish	rash

7. Sand got on it.

shell	dash

8. It swims.

lash	fish

9. It smells.

trash	flash

10. To run fast

dash	shut

Name_____

Directions for the student: **Practice reading 20 sh words on this page.** Choose 2-3 colors. Color **yes** if the sentence makes sense or could possibly be true. Color **no** if it does not make sense or could not be true.

1. A wish can crash. | yes | no |

2. She is in the shed. | yes | no |

3. Rush to get on the ship. | yes | no |

4. A dish ran to the shelf. | yes | no |

5. Al did crush the shell. | yes | no |

6. She got a rash. | yes | no |

7. Josh will splash us. | yes | no |

8. The trash smells to Trish. | yes | no |

9. Shut the fish. | yes | no |

10. The shed shot me. | yes | no |

Name_____

Directions for the student: **Practice reading 25 sh words on this page.** Choose 2-3 colors. Read each sentence or phrase. Pick the best answer and color it.

1. A truck can do it.

shop	crash

2. To end it

dish	finish

3. A plant

shell	shrub

4. Set a box on it.

shelf	mash

5. A gun did it.

shot	splash

6. Trish got on it.

cash	ship

7. It can kill Josh.

wish	shock

8. To smash to bits

shed	crush

9. She will do it.

flush	shelf

10. Sh!

hash	hush

Name_____

Directions for the student: **Practice reading 19 sh words on this page.** Choose 2-3 colors. Color *yes* if the sentence makes sense or could possibly be true. Color *no* if it does not make sense or could not be true.

1. To dash is to run fast. | yes | no |

2. She has a bad rash. | yes | no |

3. Flush the ships. | yes | no |

4. Toss Dad in the trash. | yes | no |

5. Shut off the dish. | yes | no |

6. A man got shot. | yes | no |

7. Pigs shop for shells. | yes | no |

8. Trish will splash Josh. | yes | no |

9. Ships crush fish. | yes | no |

10. A wish is on the shelf. | yes | no |

Name_____

Directions for the student: **Practice reading 22 sh words on this page.** Choose 2-3 colors. Read each sentence or phrase. Pick the best answer and color it.

1. A plant | shrub | shock |

2. Josh drops it. | shag | dish |

3. On a hot dog | relish | finish |

4. Trish bit into it. | shed | shrimp |

5. Rip into bits | shred | shun |

6. Will do | shall | ash |

7. It will get him wet. | wish | splash |

8. Soft | plush | crush |

9. It is skin. | flesh | rush |

10. A hut or cabin | shack | flush |

158

Name_____

Directions for the student: Color **yes** if the sentence makes sense or could possibly be true. Color **no** if it does not make sense or could not be true.

1. The ship will get a rash.

yes	no

2. She shops for trash.

yes	no

3. Dash to the finish line.

yes	no

4. Flush the shelf.

yes	no

5. Fish swim in sheds.

yes	no

Directions for the student: Read each sentence or phrase. Pick the best answer and color it.

6. Josh did wish for it.

lash	cash

7. It can kill.

shot	flash

8. Do it in a tub.

mash	splash

9. Set it on the shelf.

rush	dish

10. 2 vans can do it.

crash	mash

Name_____

Directions for the student: **Practice reading 23 th (voiced) words on this page.** Choose 2-3 colors. Color **yes** if the sentence makes sense or could possibly be true. Color **no** if it does not make sense or could not be true.

1. That man is Jon's father.	yes	no
2. This is his other cat.	yes	no
3. These hats yell at them.	yes	no
4. There is the red pen.	yes	no
5. Those clothes are his.	yes	no
6. Mother will bathe them.	yes	no
7. They bother his brother.	yes	no
8. Father sent them the fog.	yes	no
9. I had less than they did.	yes	no
10. Then his mother left.	yes	no

Name_____

Directions for the student: **Read 24 th (voiced) words on this page.** Choose 2-3 colors. Read each sentence or phrase. Pick the best answer and color it.

1. Mom

there	mother

2. Pants and a dress

they	clothes

3. He has a sister.

brother	then

4. Do it in a tub.

bathe	them

5. After this

then	they

6. Not these

those	then

7. Those kids

mother	them

8. To get together

gather	rather

9. Dad

these	father

10. To suds up hands

lather	this

Name_____

Directions for the student: **Practice reading 18 th (unvoiced) words on this page.** Choose 2-3 colors. Color *yes* if the sentence makes sense or could possibly be true. Color *no* if it does not make sense or could not be true.

1. Beth lost three teeth. | yes | no |

2. I think I need a bath. | yes | no |

3. A thick cloth got wet. | yes | no |

4. Ben Smith is thin. | yes | no |

5. A path can think. | yes | no |

6. Seth is with Dan. | yes | no |

7. Both dogs ran. | yes | no |

8. Thank Ann for me. | yes | no |

9. Three pigs do math. | yes | no |

10. A moth can yell. | yes | no |

         163

Name_____

Directions for the student: **Practice reading 23 th (unvoiced) words on this page.** Choose 2-3 colors. Read each sentence or phrase. Pick the best answer and color it.

1. It can be hot.

thin	bath

2. Run on it.

tenth	path

3. A neck

cloth	throat

4. Not thin

with	thick

5. 1 + 1 = 2

thump	math

6. It can be soft.

cloth	think

7. Seth's pal

Beth	bath

8. Fifth, _____

sixth	thrill

9. Not fat

tenth	thin

10. A bug

path	moth

Name_____

Directions for the student: **Practice reading 25 th (voiced and unvoiced) words on this page.** Choose 2-3 colors. Color *yes* if the sentence makes sense or could possibly be true. Color *no* if it does not make sense or could not be true.

1. This kid did the math. | yes | no |

2. They had a bath. | yes | no |

3. Throw this throat. | yes | no |

4. Mud is on that path. | yes | no |

5. His teeth will run there. | yes | no |

6. That thick cloth slept. | yes | no |

7. Beth is in the fifth van. | yes | no |

8. Three rocks can think. | yes | no |

9. Thank them for us both. | yes | no |

10. Those kids are thin. | yes | no |

th (voiced and unvoiced)

Name_____

Directions for the student: **Practice reading 30 th (voiced and unvoiced) words on this page.** Choose 2-3 colors. Read each sentence or phrase. Pick the best answer and color it.

1. This and that	both / thump
2. I bit it with these.	throat / teeth
3. It will get mud off.	thin / bath
4. Clothes are from it.	cloth / think
5. A mind will do this.	think / tenth
6. To toss	thank / throw
7. Mom, Dad, and brother	three / then
8. A cloth can be it.	both / thick
9. Dan likes to do it.	there / math
10. Beth is this.	thin / those

Name_____

Directions for the student: Color **yes** if the sentence makes sense or could possibly be true. Color **no** if it does not make sense or could not be true.

1. Moths bathe in tubs. | yes | no |

2. Both of them did math. | yes | no |

3. Clothes can think. | yes | no |

4. Thank my thin brother. | yes | no |

5. Throw mother's teeth. | yes | no |

Directions for the student: Read each sentence or phrase. Pick the best answer and color it.

6. Father thanks her. | brother | Beth |

7. Next to lips | bother | teeth |

8. A neck | lather | throat |

9. Get them on. | paths | clothes |

10. They will do it. | those | think |

     167

Name_____

Directions for the student: **Practice reading 23 ch words on this page.** Choose 2-3 colors. Color **yes** if the sentence makes sense or could possibly be true. Color **no** if it does not make sense or could not be true.

1. A chimp has six chins. | yes | no |

2. Chuck and Chad chat. | yes | no |

3. French cats do chores. | yes | no |

4. A child sits on a bench. | yes | no |

5. Chip's job is on a ranch. | yes | no |

6. Munch on chips for lunch. | yes | no |

7. Chad will punch the sun. | yes | no |

8. Chop up his chin. | yes | no |

9. He is such a bad child. | yes | no |

10. Chimps pinch chicks. | yes | no |

Name_____

Directions for the student: **Practice reading 23 ch words on this page.** Choose 2-3 colors. Read each sentence or phrase. Pick the best answer and color it.

1. Can spend a lot

rich	chest

2. To get cold

chat	chill

3. He is the best.

bench	champ

4. A fist can do it.

punch	chop

5. A snack

child	chips

6. It has fluff on it.

check	chick

7. Chad did bump his.

chop	chin

8. A kid

chip	child

9. Do it to skin.

pinch	inch

10. Chuck's had chips.

lunch	belch

Name_____

Directions for the student: **Practice reading 15 tch words on this page.** Choose 2-3 colors. Color *yes* if the sentence makes sense or could possibly be true. Color *no* if it does not make sense or could not be true.

1. Scratch my back. | yes | no |

2. Dad's socks match. | yes | no |

3. His crutch bit me. | yes | no |

4. Scratch the itch. | yes | no |

5. Stretch the ditch. | yes | no |

6. Ketchup is in the kitchen. | yes | no |

7. The witch had black on. | yes | no |

8. Mitch and I switch hats. | yes | no |

9. He can catch a ditch. | yes | no |

10. Kids hatch from eggs. | yes | no |

Name_____

Directions for the student: **Practice reading 23 tch words on this page.** Choose 2-3 colors. Read each sentence or phrase. Pick the best answer and color it.

1. Hands can do it.

batch	catch

2. Has on black

ditch	witch

3. Cats do it.

scratch	patch

4. A chick from an egg

hatch	fetch

5. A man

snatch	Mitch

6. Scratch it.

dutch	itch

7. Stitch it on a rip.

pitch	patch

8. Helps Dan's bad leg

ditch	crutch

9. A dog gets the stick.

fetch	hatch

10. Mitch lit it.

scratch	match

Name_____

Directions for the student: **Practice reading 19 ch/ tch words on this page.** Choose 2-3 colors. Color *yes* if the sentence makes sense or could possibly be true. Color *no* if it does not make sense or could not be true.

1. He can sketch a witch. | yes | no |

2. Crunch the chips. | yes | no |

3. The branch has an itch. | yes | no |

4. Dogs can fetch sticks. | yes | no |

5. I had a cheese sandwich. | yes | no |

6. Chill the spinach. | yes | no |

7. He is such a rich man. | yes | no |

8. Stitch me to the porch. | yes | no |

9. Chuck went to church. | yes | no |

10. Chimps hatch from eggs. | yes | no |

Name_____

Directions for the student: **Practice reading 23 ch / tch words on this page.** Choose 2-3 colors. Read each sentence or phrase. Pick the best answer and color it.

1. It can itch.

snatch	chin

2. Steps go up to it.

porch	pitch

3. It will fix a rip.

batch	patch

4. Did pick

chose	ditch

5. Chop with it.

hatchet	inch

6. A bit fat

dutch	chubby

7. Kids do it.

chick	chat

8. To run to catch him

chase	ditch

9. Do not do on a test.

hitch	cheat

10. To go get

such	fetch

Name_____

Directions for the student: Color **yes** if the sentence makes sense or could possibly be true. Color **no** if it does not make sense or could not be true.

1. Stitch the bench.

yes	no

2. Switch cheeks with me.

yes	no

3. Stretch the chest.

yes	no

4. Munch on the crutch.

yes	no

5. Chad can catch a cold.

yes	no

Directions for the student: Read each sentence or phrase. Pick the best answer and color it.

6. To hit

punch	snatch

7. It can be lit.

match	chill

8. Chips and sandwich

lunch	patch

9. Has a black hat

chick	witch

10. Do to an itch

scratch	ditch

Name_____

Directions for the student: **Practice reading 15 wh words on this page.** Choose 2-3 colors. Color *yes* if the sentence makes sense or could possibly be true. Color *no* if it does not make sense or could not be true.

1. Wheels can ask why. | yes | no |

2. Whales whip dogs. | yes | no |

3. Rocks whisper. | yes | no |

4. I see which bed is white. | yes | no |

5. Tell me when I can go. | yes | no |

6. Find where the box is. | yes | no |

7. Dad's whiskers pick me. | yes | no |

8. A whistle has wheels. | yes | no |

9. He whines and whimpers. | yes | no |

10. Sit for a while. | yes | no |

wh (as in **wh**ip)

Name_____

Directions for the student: **Practice reading 20 wh words on this page.** Choose 2-3 colors. Read each sentence or phrase. Pick the best answer and color it.

1. It is a big fish.	whip	whale

2. Time tells it.	when	whine

3. Shhhh!	wheat	whisper

4. On cats	whiskers	whips

5. On a bus	whales	wheels

6. Ask it.	why	whisk

7. Lips do it.	whip	whistle

8. To hit	whack	which

9. To spin	whirl	why

10. A bit of time	what	while

Name_____

Directions for the student: **Practice reading 12 wh words on this page.** Choose 2-3 colors. Color *yes* if the sentence makes sense or could possibly be true. Color *no* if it does not make sense or could not be true.

1. Whiskers are on wheels. | yes | no |

2. I see where the box is. | yes | no |

3. Black is white. | yes | no |

4. He bit into a wheat bun. | yes | no |

5. Sam can whistle. | yes | no |

6. He ran while I sat. | yes | no |

7. Pigs whack whales. | yes | no |

8. A whisper is a yell. | yes | no |

9. Pick which pen is red. | yes | no |

10. Ask him why he did it. | yes | no |

Name_____

Directions for the student: **Practice reading 20 wh words on this page.** Choose 2-3 colors. Read each sentence or phrase. Pick the best answer and color it.

1. To beg

whine	white

2. Lips can do it.

when	whisper

3. Hit with it.

wheel	whip

4. On a map

where	why

5. Dan can do it.

whistle	wheat

6. Al's socks

wheel	white

7. It can swim.

whale	whisker

8. Kids ask it.

whip	why

9. On a man

whack	whiskers

10. Ben can fix it.

wheel	what

Name_____

Directions for the student: **Practice reading 12 wh words on this page.** Choose 2-3 colors. Color *yes* if the sentence makes sense or could possibly be true. Color *no* if it does not make sense or could not be true.

1. A whale asks why. | yes | no

2. Milk is white. | yes | no

3. Eggs can whistle. | yes | no

4. Whales ask, "What?" | yes | no

5. Whip the eggs. | yes | no

6. A van has wheels. | yes | no

7. Tell which hat is Jim's. | yes | no

8. Tom whines. | yes | no

9. Wheat is a plant. | yes | no

10. Mom has whiskers. | yes | no

Name_____

Directions for the student: **Practice reading 20 wh words on this page.** Choose 2-3 colors. Read each sentence or phrase. Pick the best answer and color it.

1. It has fins. | whale | whip |

2. Not a yell | what | whisper |

3. Can feel picky. | whisker | whistle |

4. To twirl | whirl | whine |

5. Not black | wheeze | white |

6. Hammers can do it. | wheel | whack |

7. Men can sip it. | whiskey | why |

8. A pup can do it. | when | whimper |

9. A bun can be it. | wheat | whistle |

10. Say to get to stop. | whoa | what |

Name_____

Directions for the student: Color **yes** if the sentence makes sense or could possibly be true. Color **no** if it does not make sense or could not be true.

1. A whale has wheels. | yes | no |

2. Ed's whiskers are white. | yes | no |

3. Wheat whispers. | yes | no |

4. The wheel whips Al. | yes | no |

5. Jim can whistle. | yes | no |

Directions for the student: Read each sentence or phrase. Pick the best answer and color it.

6. Jan's top is it. | white | whip |

7. On a man | whiskers | whisk |

8. Ask it. | when | whimper |

9. It is wet. | what | whale |

10. To hit | wheat | whack |

Name

Directions for the student: **Practice reading 12 ph words on this page.** Choose 2-3 colors. Color *yes* if the sentence makes sense or could possibly be true. Color *no* if it does not make sense or could not be true.

1. Phil is on the phone. | yes | no |

2. Dan won a trophy. | yes | no |

3. Snap a photo of us. | yes | no |

4. Phonics is math. | yes | no |

5. Ralph is a girl. | yes | no |

6. A box is a sphere. | yes | no |

7. A dolphin can trip. | yes | no |

8. We do graphs in math. | yes | no |

9. "M" is in the alphabet. | yes | no |

10. My nephew is a gopher. | yes | no |

Name_____

Directions for the student: **Practice reading 22 ph words on this page.** Choose 2-3 colors. Read each sentence or phrase. Pick the best answer and color it.

1. A-b-c's

alphabet	graph

2. A ball

sphere	phrase

3. Plot it in math.

graph	phone

4. To win in the end

triumph	phonics

5. It digs.

dolphin	gopher

6. Ralph chats on it.

photo	phone

7. Has an uncle.

phrase	nephew

8. It swims.

dolphin	hyphen

9. See on a phone.

triumph	photos

10. He went to bed.

phonics	Ralph

ph (as in gra**ph**)

Name_____

Directions for the student: **Practice reading 18 ph words on this page.** Choose 2-3 colors. Color *yes* if the sentence makes sense or could possibly be true. Color *no* if it does not make sense or could not be true.

1. An elephant has fins.	yes	no
2. Joseph is his nephew.	yes	no
3. I had a photo of Ralph.	yes	no
4. A gopher won a trophy.	yes	no
5. Phil prints the alphabet.	yes	no
6. Get pills at a pharmacy.	yes	no
7. Phil opens the pamphlet.	yes	no
8. Murphy went to bed.	yes	no
9. Dolphins visit orphans.	yes	no
10. Ralph has Phil's phone.	yes	no

Name_____

Directions for the student: **Practice reading 22 ph words on this page.** Choose 2-3 colors. Read each sentence or phrase. Pick the best answer and color it.

1. No mom or dad

orphan	sphere

2. The best get it.

trophy	gopher

3. My sister's kid

nephew	phrase

4. Ralph's pal

phonics	Joseph

5. Dad lost his.

dolphin	phone

6. A doctor check-up

physical	hyphen

7. Kids will say it.

alphabet	phase

8. Not big

elephant	gopher

9. It is on a road.

triumph	asphalt

10. See his photo.

sphere	Phil

Name_____

Directions for the student: **Practice reading 14 ph words on this page.** Choose 2-3 colors. Color **yes** if the sentence makes sense or could possibly be true. Color **no** if it does not make sense or could not be true.

1. I will triumph in the end. | yes | no |

2. Murphy got a big trophy. | yes | no |

3. An elephant has a phone. | yes | no |

4. He visits an orphanage. | yes | no |

5. A prophet predicts. | yes | no |

6. The alphabet is letters. | yes | no |

7. It is a photo of Joseph. | yes | no |

8. Pass Ralph a pamphlet. | yes | no |

9. Go to the pharmacy. | yes | no |

10. Gophers pet cats. | yes | no |

ph (as in gra**ph**)

Name_____

Directions for the student: **Practice reading 22 ph words on this page.** Choose 2-3 colors. Read each sentence or phrase. Pick the best answer and color it.

1. Has legs

| pharmacy | elephant |

2. A shape

| orphan | sphere |

3. In a pocket

| phone | elephant |

4. Helps to read.

| phonics | triumph |

5. It is wet.

| dolphin | phantom |

6. Smile for it.

| physical | photo |

7. A winner gets it.

| trophy | graph |

8. Not big

| gopher | elephant |

9. Phil adopts him.

| Ralph | pamphlet |

10. His dad

| sphere | Phil |

Name_____

Directions for the student: Color **yes** if the sentence makes sense or could possibly be true. Color **no** if it does not make sense or could not be true.

1. Phil is in a class photo. | yes | no |

2. My nephew got a trophy. | yes | no |

3. Elephants snap photos. | yes | no |

4. A phone is a sphere. | yes | no |

5. Ralph is at a pharmacy. | yes | no |

Directions for the student: Read each sentence or phrase. Pick the best answer and color it.

6. Call on it. | graph | phone |

7. A ball is it. | sphere | gopher |

8. My nephew | Joseph | phonics |

9. Can adopt him. | orphan | photo |

10. Will not swim | dolphin | elephant |

Name_____

Directions for the student: **Practice reading 20 ar words on this page.** Choose 2-3 colors. Color **yes** if the sentence makes sense or could possibly be true. Color **no** if it does not make sense or could not be true.

1. The car will not start. | yes | no |

2. A farm is in the cart. | yes | no |

3. Dogs bark in the yard. | yes | no |

4. Part of the test is hard. | yes | no |

5. A dart hit the target. | yes | no |

6. He runs far in the park. | yes | no |

7. An arm is in the jar. | yes | no |

8. A shark is in the barn. | yes | no |

9. Mark sent a card. | yes | no |

10. Carl is smart. | yes | no |

Name_____

Directions for the student: **Practice reading 25 ar words on this page.** Choose 2-3 colors. Read each sentence or phrase. Pick the best answer and color it.

1. Get in it and go.

car	arm

2. It has a lid.

card	jar

3. Carl can't see in it.

dark	bark

4. Do it to a car.

hard	park

5. Can be on a flag.

star	far

6. Mark sent it to Carl.

card	park

7. It is on a farm.

jar	barn

8. A pig is on it.

farm	arm

9. A dog will do it.

part	bark

10. Part of it can bend.

yard	arm

Name_____

Directions for the student: **Practice reading 23 ar words on this page.** Choose 2-3 colors. Color *yes* if the sentence makes sense or could possibly be true. Color *no* if it does not make sense or could not be true.

	yes	no
1. Karen will carry the bag.	yes	no
2. Larry ate the barrel.	yes	no
3. Harry will munch carrots.	yes	no
4. Clare is at the library.	yes	no
5. Parrots share arrows.	yes	no
6. Mary will carry the van.	yes	no
7. Gary scares carrots.	yes	no
8. Kids marry parents.	yes	no
9. Sharon gave to charity.	yes	no
10. Harry will marry Carrie.	yes	no

Name_____

Directions for the student: **Practice reading 26 ar words on this page.** Choose 2-3 colors. Read each sentence or phrase. Pick the best answer and color it.

1. Do it to a baby.	carry	marry
2. Mary went here.	library	arrow
3. Sharon's pet	parrot	spare
4. It is a plant.	barrel	carrot
5. Harry and Clare do it.	marry	scarce
6. Not wide	narrow	carry
7. A mom or dad	parrot	parent
8. Gary shot it.	arrow	library
9. An extra, in case	spare	carrot
10. Limited and rare	fare	scarce

ar sounded (as in c**ar** and c**ar**ry)

Name_____

Directions for the student: **Practice reading 26 ar words on this page.** Choose 2-3 colors. Color *yes* if the sentence makes sense or could possibly be true. Color *no* if it does not make sense or could not be true.

1. Mark and Karen marry. | yes | no

2. It is a narrow yard. | yes | no

3. Mary has a spare arm. | yes | no

4. Larry's car will not start. | yes | no

5. Carrots run in the park. | yes | no

6. Carry the barn in a car. | yes | no

7. Sharon's dog barks. | yes | no

8. An arrow can do harm. | yes | no

9. Gary is Harry's parent. | yes | no

10. A parrot parks the car. | yes | no

Name_____

Directions for the student: **Practice reading 34 ar words on this page.** Choose 2-3 colors. Read each sentence or phrase. Pick the best answer and color it.

1. It is on a farm.

scarce	barn

2. Mark bit part of it.

carrot	far

3. Carry it with care.

library	jar

4. A path can be it.

star	narrow

5. Get in it.

parent	cart

6. Larry's is dark red.

carry	car

7. Mark and Mary do it.

marry	hard

8. Harry is in his.

carrot	yard

9. Mark an "X" on it.

care	card

10. A part of Sharon

barrel	arm

Name_____

Directions for the student: Color **yes** if the sentence makes sense or could possibly be true. Color **no** if it does not make sense or could not be true.

1. Mark will carry the jar. | yes | no |

2. Parents bark. | yes | no |

3. Carl shares his carrots. | yes | no |

4. He is scared of the dark. | yes | no |

5. A parrot can park cars. | yes | no |

Directions for the student: Read each sentence or phrase. Pick the best answer and color it.

6. Not soft | marry | hard |

7. It can go and stop. | barrel | car |

8. Hits a target | arrow | harm |

9. Up if it is dark | stars | stares |

10. Do it to a box. | carry | farm |

Name_____

Directions for the student: **Practice reading 23 er words on this page.** Choose 2-3 colors. Color *yes* if the sentence makes sense or could possibly be true. Color *no* if it does not make sense or could not be true.

1. Her mother had butter. | yes | no |

2. Send a letter to Amber. | yes | no |

3. A butler serves dinner. | yes | no |

4. Tell her to do it later. | yes | no |

5. Bert gets on my nerves. | yes | no |

6. Her zipper is never stuck. | yes | no |

7. His sister got fatter. | yes | no |

8. Pepper the runner's hat. | yes | no |

9. Winter is never cold. | yes | no |

10. Rubber is clever. | yes | no |

Name_____

Directions for the student: **Practice reading 27 er words on this page.** Choose 2-3 colors. Read each sentence or phrase. Pick the best answer and color it.

1. The runner is it.

suffer	winner

2. A stamp is on it.

helper	letter

3. Mother serves it.

dinner	fatter

4. On my paper

tender	sticker

5. Not ever

clerk	never

6. Set it.

tiger	timer

7. Amber prints on it.

paper	serve

8. It can be hot.

winter	summer

9. It can melt.

pepper	butter

10. It is Bert's.

later	hammer

Name_____

Directions for the student: **Practice reading 14 er words on this page.** Choose 2-3 colors. Color **yes** if the sentence makes sense or could possibly be true. Color **no** if it does not make sense or could not be true.

1. The sun is very hot. | yes | no |

2. Jerry is in America. | yes | no |

3. The sad man is merry. | yes | no |

4. Sit there. | yes | no |

5. A cherry is red. | yes | no |

6. The rock bit a berry. | yes | no |

7. Perry's rash is terrible. | yes | no |

8. Derek is in bed. | yes | no |

9. Jerry and Terry are twins. | yes | no |

10. I see where Eric is. | yes | no |

Name_____

Directions for the student: **Practice reading 24 er words on this page.** Choose 2-3 colors. Read each sentence or phrase. Pick the best answer and color it.

1. A map tells it.

merry	where

2. Yum!

very	berry

3. Very bad

there	terrible

4. Eric bit it.

cherry	where

5. Not here

there	very

6. He sat next to Derek.

cherry	Perry

7. Pick it.

berry	terrible

8. Terry is it.

merry	very

9. It has a pit.

there	cherry

10. Ask it.

where	berry

Name_____

Directions for the student: **Practice reading 28 er words on this page.** Choose 2-3 colors. Color **yes** if the sentence makes sense or could possibly be true. Color **no** if it does not make sense or could not be true.

1. Bert's sister left America. | yes | no |

2. Eric has a terrible temper. | yes | no |

3. Tell Amber where to go. | yes | no |

4. A cherry bit her finger. | yes | no |

5. Derek butters his slipper. | yes | no |

6. It is a very hot summer. | yes | no |

7. I see where her father is. | yes | no |

8. Terry is very merry. | yes | no |

9. Jerry is older than Perry. | yes | no |

10. The butler is over there. | yes | no |

Name_____

Directions for the student: **Practice reading 27 er words on this page.** Choose 2-3 colors. Read each sentence or phrase. Pick the best answer and color it.

1. Not a good job	terrible	slipper
2. It has a pit.	fatter	cherry
3. Jolly and happy	sliver	merry
4. It went off.	timer	berry
5. Derek stuck it.	very	sticker
6. Jerry will pass it.	pepper	merry
7. Eric enters it.	camper	terrible
8. Serve it later to Ed.	there	dinner
9. It is very hot.	cherry	summer
10. The best at it	expert	tender

206

Name_____

Directions for the student: Color **yes** if the sentence makes sense or could possibly be true. Color **no** if it does not make sense or could not be true.

1. Pass pepper to Derek. | yes | no |

2. Jerry had a fever. | yes | no |

3. The older man is merry. | yes | no |

4. Her temper is very bad. | yes | no |

5. Eric had a terrible fever. | yes | no |

Directions for the student: Read each sentence or phrase. Pick the best answer and color it.

6. Serve it to Bert. | under | cherry |

7. Six and ten | numbers | inner |

8. It can go up. | zipper | merry |

9. Where to sit | there | liver |

10. Send it. | berry | letter |

Name_____

Directions for the student: **Practice reading 18 ir words on this page.** Choose 2-3 colors. Color *yes* if the sentence makes sense or could possibly be true. Color *no* if it does not make sense or could not be true.

1. Let the girls go first.	yes	no
2. Mud is wet dirt.	yes	no
3. A bird chirps.	yes	no
4. A girl can be thirsty.	yes	no
5. Stir the shirt.	yes	no
6. Let's go to the circus.	yes	no
7. The girl's skirt is red.	yes	no
8. Dirt is on the shirts.	yes	no
9. Ed's first and I am third.	yes	no
10. Kirk will squirt Jill.	yes	no

Name_____

Directions for the student: **Practice reading 23 ir words on this page.** Choose 2-3 colors. Read each sentence or phrase. Pick the best answer and color it.

1. Not a boy

girl	firm

2. In a nest

birth	bird

3. Mud is from it

flirt	dirt

4. First, second…

third	firm

5. To mix

skirt	stir

6. A bird will do it.

chirp	dirt

7. A girl had it on.

Kirk	skirt

8. Not soft

firm	sir

9. To spin

twirl	third

10. Dad's is red.

skirt	shirt

Name_____

Directions for the student: **Practice reading 16 ir words on this page.** Choose 2-3 colors. Color *yes* if the sentence makes sense or could possibly be true. Color *no* if it does not make sense or could not be true.

1. The bird had on a skirt. | yes | no |

2. His shirt had dirt on it. | yes | no |

3. Kirk is first. | yes | no |

4. A girl can flirt. | yes | no |

5. I had a thirst for dirt. | yes | no |

6. Stir it to mix it up. | yes | no |

7. The third circle is red. | yes | no |

8. A rock has a birthday. | yes | no |

9. Pigs chirp. | yes | no |

10. Tell Dad, "Yes, sir." | yes | no |

Name_____

Directions for the student: **Practice reading 24 ir words on this page.** Choose 2-3 colors. Read each sentence or phrase. Pick the best answer and color it.

1. It can chirp.

bird	girl

2. Plant in it.

skirt	dirt

3. Kirk did rip his.

birth	shirt

4. To mix

stir	chirp

5. 10, 20, ...

thirty	girl

6. It is for a girl.

skirt	dirt

7. In front

first	firm

8. An "O" is this.

third	circle

9. A man

sir	bird

10. He is thirsty.

birth	Kirk

Name_____

Directions for the student: **Practice reading 18 ir words on this page.** Choose 2-3 colors. Color **yes** if the sentence makes sense or could possibly be true. Color **no** if it does not make sense or could not be true.

1. It is his first birthday. | yes | no |

2. Plant birds in the dirt. | yes | no |

3. A girl zips the skirt. | yes | no |

4. Stir the circle. | yes | no |

5. Birds yell "Yes, sir!" | yes | no |

6. The third kid is first. | yes | no |

7. Shirts fit hands. | yes | no |

8. Giraffes chirp. | yes | no |

9. Kirk digs in the dirt. | yes | no |

10. Ed had a squirt gun. | yes | no |

Name_____

Directions for the student: **Practice reading 23 ir words on this page.** Choose 2-3 colors. Read each
sentence or phrase. Pick the best answer and color it.

1. Kirk scrubs it off.

dirt	third

2. It has a pocket.

shirt	firm

3. Has a long neck

birth	giraffe

4. Dad is it.

stir	thirty

5. Jan, Pam, and Ann

girls	sir

6. Bill did it to Bob.

squirt	dirt

7. Do it to batter

stir	flirt

8. The girls went to it.

circus	circle

9. Not for a man

sir	skirt

10. Girls can do it.

firm	flirt

214

Name_____

Directions for the student: Color **yes** if the sentence makes sense or could possibly be true. Color **no** if it does not make sense or could not be true.

1. Skirts get thirsty.	yes	no

2. Kirk's shirt had dirt on it.	yes	no

3. The girl stirs a pot.	yes	no

4. Birds chirp "Yes, sir".	yes	no

5. We will squirt Al first.	yes	no

Directions for the student: Read each sentence or phrase. Pick the best answer and color it.

6. A man	stir	sir

7. Not first	chirp	third

8. A bed can be it.	firm	girl

9. A robin	bird	shirt

10. Mom mops it up.	thirst	dirt

Name_____

Directions for the student: **Practice reading 21 or words on this page.** Choose 2-3 colors. Color *yes* if the sentence makes sense or could possibly be true. Color *no* if it does not make sense or could not be true.

1. Doris sat on the porch. | yes | no |

2. Fix pork and corn for us. | yes | no |

3. We can't afford a horse. | yes | no |

4. The lamp cord is sore. | yes | no |

5. The cork bit the fork. | yes | no |

6. Jan's shorts are torn. | yes | no |

7. Mort's horse ran fast. | yes | no |

8. His pastor is short. | yes | no |

9. Norm snores. | yes | no |

10. Go to the store for milk. | yes | no |

Name_____

Directions for the student: **Practice reading 23 or words on this page.** Choose 2-3 colors. Read each sentence or phrase. Pick the best answer and color it.

1. Sit on it.

for	horse

2. Steps go up to it.

pork	porch

3. Get it from a plant.

torn	corn

4. A cut on my leg is it.

sort	sore

5. A lamp has it.

cord	corn

6. Norm did drop his.

ford	fork

7. Mort got wet in it.

storm	tore

8. In an apple

cord	core

9. Had it on

wore	porch

10. Doris shops at it.

born	store

Name_____

Directions for the student: **Practice reading 20 or words on this page.** Choose 2-3 colors. Color **yes** if the sentence makes sense or could possibly be true. Color **no** if it does not make sense or could not be true.

1. A horn can be sore. | yes | no |

2. It is a short test. | yes | no |

3. Mort trips on the cord. | yes | no |

4. This is Norm's fork. | yes | no |

5. Doris is as short as Al. | yes | no |

6. Pigs do chores for us. | yes | no |

7. He tore the store. | yes | no |

8. Mom will get more pork. | yes | no |

9. Norm will go up north. | yes | no |

10. A horse wore shorts. | yes | no |

Name_____

Directions for the student: **Practice reading 23 or words on this page.** Choose 2-3 colors. Read each sentence or phrase. Pick the best answer and color it.

1. Stick it into ham. | fork | horn |

2. A plug is at the end. | cork | cord |

3. His dad will do it. | snore | sore |

4. Mort sat on it. | torn | porch |

5. Had it on | cord | wore |

6. A kid can be it. | short | form |

7. Norm had to do it. | horn | chore |

8. Up, on a map | north | born |

9. I did it to my test. | pork | tore |

10. On a fork | born | corn |

Name_____

Directions for the student: **Practice reading 18 or words on this page.** Choose 2-3 colors. Color **yes** if the sentence makes sense or could possibly be true. Color **no** if it does not make sense or could not be true.

1. He tore his shorts. | yes | no |

2. The pork is for Mort. | yes | no |

3. A horse was born. | yes | no |

4. Cut up the porch. | yes | no |

5. Doris went up north. | yes | no |

6. I tore the corn. | yes | no |

7. We sell storms. | yes | no |

8. I forgot to do chores. | yes | no |

9. Norm has a sore leg. | yes | no |

10. Pigs snort. | yes | no |

Name_____

Directions for the student: **Practice reading 25 or words on this page.** Choose 2-3 colors. Read each sentence or phrase. Pick the best answer and color it.

1. It can be short.

snore	cord

2. He will do it to Doris.

ignore	form

3. It left my mind.

forgot	sore

4. Had it on

north	wore

5. Mort will do it.

snore	fork

6. It runs fast.

short	horse

7. Norm's truck has it.

horn	chore

8. Had it with my pork.

torn	corn

9. Get wet in it.

born	storm

10. It will get better.

sore	bore

Name_____

Directions for the student: Color **yes** if the sentence makes sense or could possibly be true. Color **no** if it does not make sense or could not be true.

1. A store snores. | yes | no |

2. Forks do chores. | yes | no |

3. The porch forgot. | yes | no |

4. Norm ignores Mort. | yes | no |

5. It is a short cord. | yes | no |

Directions for the student: Read each sentence or phrase. Pick the best answer and color it.

6. In a can | score | corn |

7. A job for a kid | chore | porch |

8. It gets wet. | shore | snore |

9. Did rip | ford | tore |

10. That kid is it. | core | short |

     223

Name_____

Directions for the student: **Practice reading 17 ur words on this page.** Choose 2-3 colors. Color *yes* if the sentence makes sense or could possibly be true. Color *no* if it does not make sense or could not be true.

1. The nurse had a purse. | yes | no |

2. Turn off the fan. | yes | no |

3. Kurt sat on the curb. | yes | no |

4. It hurts to burp. | yes | no |

5. To murder is to kill. | yes | no |

6. A pig has purple curls. | yes | no |

7. A turkey can be fat. | yes | no |

8. Burns can hurt. | yes | no |

9. It is Burke's turn. | yes | no |

10. A turtle has fur. | yes | no |

Name_____

Directions for the student: **Practice reading 23 ur words on this page.** Choose 2-3 colors. Read each sentence or phrase. Pick the best answer and color it.

1. A kid can do it.

burst	burp

2. Mom's is big.

purse	curb

3. To kill

curl	murder

4. On a dog

curb	fur

5. A church can do it.

burn	turn

6. She helps the sick.

curl	nurse

7. A bubble can do it.

burst	purr

8. Kurt's cap is it.

purple	hurt

9. Go left.

burp	turn

10. Burns do this.

hurt	fur

Name_____

Directions for the student: **Practice reading 22 ur words on this page.** Choose 2-3 colors. Color **yes** if the sentence makes sense or could possibly be true. Color **no** if it does not make sense or could not be true.

1. Fur can burst. | yes | no |

2. Curtis ate turkey. | yes | no |

3. Curbs purr. | yes | no |

4. A purse is for burps. | yes | no |

5. A nurse helps hurt kids. | yes | no |

6. Wilbur burns a log. | yes | no |

7. Kurt curls a curb. | yes | no |

8. Fur can burp. | yes | no |

9. A nurse is purple. | yes | no |

10. Burt murders a curl. | yes | no |

Name_____

Directions for the student: **Practice reading 21 ur words on this page.** Choose 2-3 colors. Read each sentence or phrase. Pick the best answer and color it.

1. Ann's dress is it.

| burp | purple |

2. Me, then you

| turns | burn |

3. It gobbles.

| fur | turkey |

4. Cats do it.

| purr | burst |

5. Helps the sick

| burn | nurse |

6. A cut on a leg

| curl | hurt |

7. Mom has gum in it.

| purse | murder |

8. Go the other way

| turn | purr |

9. Kurt will not do it.

| curse | blur |

10. It can be soft.

| curb | fur |

Name_____

Directions for the student: **Practice reading 18 ur words on this page.** Choose 2-3 colors. Color **yes** if the sentence makes sense or could possibly be true. Color **no** if it does not make sense or could not be true.

1. Turn the burner off. | yes | no |

2. It is bad to curse. | yes | no |

3. Mom's purse hurts. | yes | no |

4. A turkey has fur. | yes | no |

5. A nurse helps Burt. | yes | no |

6. Curbs are purple. | yes | no |

7. The sun can burn Curtis. | yes | no |

8. Dogs purr. | yes | no |

9. Burke burps his van. | yes | no |

10. Pigs turn into turkeys. | yes | no |

Name_____

Directions for the student: **Practice reading 23 ur words on this page.** Choose 2-3 colors. Read each sentence or phrase. Pick the best answer and color it.

1. Not for men | burst | purse |

2. A cut on the skin | purr | hurts |

3. Black on Kurt's cat | fur | burst |

4. Helps us get well. | nurse | murder |

5. Ann cut them off. | curb | curls |

6. Do it with a gun. | blur | murder |

7. Bubbles do it. | burst | curse |

8. On a bun | burger | burp |

9. Its leg is hurt. | turkey | purple |

10. Wilbur will do it. | burp | church |

Name_____

Directions for the student: Color **yes** if the sentence makes sense or could possibly be true. Color **no** if it does not make sense or could not be true.

1. Turtles purr.

yes	no

2. Curl the burp.

yes	no

3. Turn Kurt into a turkey.

yes	no

4. The nurse got hurt.

yes	no

5. Dad turns the burgers.

yes	no

Directions for the student: Read each sentence or phrase. Pick the best answer and color it.

6. To get hurt

fur	injure

7. A cut can do it.

blur	hurt

8. Can be on a nurse

curls	burst

9. Mom did burn it.

curb	turkey

10. Can be purple

turn	purse

ANSWER KEY - WORKBOOK A

Page 1	Page 2	Page 3	Page 4	Page 5	Page 6
yes	add	yes	map	no	cat
no	ham	yes	rag	yes	rat
no	rat	no	sad	no	damp
yes	gas	no	cat	yes	van
yes	bag	yes	Sam	yes	brat
yes	van	yes	cab	yes	hand
no	jam	yes	cap	yes	man
no	clap	no	pals	no	cap
yes	Sam	no	hands	no	fat
yes	Dan	no	van	yes	bag

Page 7	Page 9	Page 10	Page 11	Page 12	Page 13
1. no	1. no	1. bed	1. no	1. vest	1. yes
2. no	2. yes	2. vest	2. yes	2. peck	2. yes
3. yes	3. yes	3. hen	3. yes	3. nest	3. yes
4. no	4. no	4. beg	4. no	4. Ken	4. no
5. yes	5. yes	5. wept	5. yes	5. pen	5. no
6. map	6. yes	6. wed	6. yes	6. help	6. no
7. bag	7. yes	7. end	7. yes	7. tent	7. yes
8. hat	8. yes	8. dress	8. no	8. pet	8. no
9. rag	9. no	9. mess	9. yes	9. men	9. no
10. hands	10. no	10. pet	10. yes	10. desk	10. yes

Page 14	Page 15	Page 17	Page 18	Page 19	Page 20
1. dress	1. no	1. no	1. lips	1. no	1. Bill
2. slept	2. no	2. no	2. mitt	2. yes	2. mint
3. leg	3. yes	3. no	3. hill	3. yes	3. pill
4. sled	4. yes	4. yes	4. big	4. no	4. mitt
5. bells	5. no	5. yes	5. hit	5. no	5. swim
6. belt	6. pen	6. no	6. kick	6. no	6. lid
7. beg	7. leg	7. no	7. rip	7. yes	7. pins
8. help	8. belt	8. yes	8. milk	8. no	8. milk
9. rest	9. bed	9. yes	9. Rick	9. no	9. Rick
10. hen	10. jet	10. yes	10. pin	10. yes	10. kiss

Page 21	Page 22	Page 23	Page 25	Page 26	Page 27
1. yes	1. drip	1. no	1. no	1. cop	1. yes
2. no	2. pill	2. no	2. yes	2. pond	2. yes
3. yes	3. kiss	3. no	3. yes	3. doll	3. no
4. yes	4. wig	4. yes	4. yes	4. pot	4. no
5. no	5. sip	5. no	5. no	5. sock	5. yes
6. yes	6. win	6. rib	6. yes	6. mop	6. no
7. yes	7. bib	7. stick	7. yes	7. off	7. no
8. no	8. pin	8. bib	8. yes	8. spot	8. yes
9. no	9. trip	9. brick	9. no	9. rock	9. yes
10. yes	10. mints	10. hid	10. yes	10. clock	10. no

Page 28	Page 29	Page 30	Page 31	Page 33	Page 34
1. rocks	1. no	1. rock	1. no	1. no	1. mud
2. sob	2. no	2. job	2. no	2. no	2. sun
3. box	3. yes	3. sock	3. yes	3. no	3. bus
4. soft	4. no	4. cot	4. yes	4. no	4. run
5. rob	5. no	5. on	5. yes	5. yes	5. hum
6. frog	6. yes	6. rob	6. fog	6. yes	6. nut
7. Ron	7. yes	7. box	7. cot	7. no	7. mug
8. cop	8. yes	8. hog	8. dog	8. yes	8. bug
9. dots	9. yes	9. mop	9. mop	9. no	9. plug
10. job	10. no	10. log	10. clock	10. yes	10. rust

Page 35	Page 36	Page 37	Page 38	Page 39	Page 41
1. yes	1. mud	1. no	1. dug	1. yes	1. yes
2. no	2. bus	2. no	2. bug	2. no	2. no
3. yes	3. cut	3. no	3. bus	3. no	3. yes
4. no	4. sum	4. yes	4. drugs	4. yes	4. no
5. no	5. hug	5. no	5. fun	5. no	5. no
6. yes	6. bug	6. no	6. rub	6. lump	6. no
7. yes	7. drug	7. no	7. drum	7. bus	7. yes
8. no	8. mug	8. no	8. plum	8. suds	8. no
9. no	9. bun	9. yes	9. tub	9. mud	9. yes
10. no	10. mud	10. yes	10. dump	10. bug	10. no

Page 42	Page 43	Page 44	Page 45	Page 46	Page 47
1. cake	1. no	1. lake	1. yes	1. names	1. yes
2. lake	2. yes	2. hate	2. no	2. game	2. no
3. cane	3. no	3. wave	3. yes	3. cape	3. no
4. wave	4. yes	4. take	4. no	4. bare	4. no
5. plane	5. no	5. cave	5. no	5. cave	5. yes
6. Jane	6. yes	6. sale	6. no	6. wade	6. snake
7. vase	7. no	7. cake	7. yes	7. snake	7. game
8. tape	8. no	8. date	8. yes	8. wake	8. brake
9. gate	9. no	9. grape	9. yes	9. blame	9. Jake
10. rake	10. no	10. bake	10. no	10. flame	10. lake

Page 49	Page 50	Page 51	Page 52	Page 53	Page 54
1. yes	1. hair	1. yes	1. paint	1. yes	1. fail
2. no	2. pail	2. no	2. nail	2. no	2. hair
3. no	3. tail	3. no	3. mail	3. no	3. maid
4. no	4. nail	4. yes	4. pain	4. no	4. rain
5. yes	5. jail	5. no	5. air	5. no	5. waist
6. no	6. stair	6. no	6. stain	6. no	6. paid
7. no	7. train	7. yes	7. stair	7. yes	7. tail
8. yes	8. paint	8. yes	8. brain	8. no	8. pail
9. yes	9. stain	9. no	9. pair	9. yes	9. trail
10. no	10. wait	10. yes	10. train	10. no	10. jail

Page 55	Page 57	Page 58	Page 59	Page 60	Page 61
1. no	1. no	1. clay	1. no	1. gray	1. yes
2. no	2. yes	2. pray	2. yes	2. stay	2. yes
3. no	3. no	3. lay	3. no	3. play	3. yes
4. yes	4. yes	4. stay	4. no	4. tray	4. yes
5. yes	5. yes	5. pay	5. yes	5. pray	5. no
6. mail	6. no	6. hay	6. no	6. lay	6. yes
7. braid	7. yes	7. ray	7. no	7. Ray	7. no
8. drain	8. yes	8. play	8. yes	8. clay	8. yes
9. train	9. yes	9. say	9. no	9. say	9. yes
10. brain	10. no	10. Jay	10. yes	10. hay	10. no

Page 62	Page 63	Page 65	Page 66	Page 67	Page 68
1. Jay	1. yes	1. yes	1. seed	1. yes	1. heels
2. pray	2. yes	2. yes	2. weep	2. no	2. sleep
3. day	3. yes	3. no	3. tree	3. yes	3. keep
4. tray	4. yes	4. yes	4. bee	4. no	4. Lee
5. yay	5. no	5. no	5. peel	5. yes	5. weed
6. may	6. Jay	6. no	6. jeep	6. yes	6. tree
7. play	7. spray	7. no	7. weed	7. no	7. feet
8. spray	8. tray	8. yes	8. free	8. yes	8. steep
9. okay	9. gray	9. yes	9. feet	9. yes	9. teen
10. gray	10. say	10. no	10. need	10. yes	10. breeze

Page 69	Page 70	Page 71	Page 73	Page 74	Page 75
1. no	1. sweep	1. no	1. no	1. meat	1. yes
2. yes	2. tree	2. yes	2. yes	2. beat	2. yes
3. no	3. sleep	3. yes	3. no	3. leak	3. yes
4. yes	4. need	4. no	4. yes	4. mean	4. yes
5. yes	5. green	5. yes	5. yes	5. heat	5. yes
6. no	6. sneeze	6. steer	6. yes	6. read	6. no
7. yes	7. beef	7. sleep	7. no	7. seat	7. no
8. yes	8. feet	8. deer	8. yes	8. team	8. no
9. no	9. greed	9. feet	9. yes	9. heal	9. no
10. yes	10. bleed	10. heel	10. no	10. tea	10. no

Page 76	Page 77	Page 78	Page 79	Page 81	Page 82
1. beak	1. no	1. mean	1. yes	1. yes	1. money
2. hear	2. no	2. jeans	2. no	2. yes	2. key
3. beans	3. no	3. ear	3. no	3. yes	3. tummy
4. jeans	4. yes	4. team	4. yes	4. no	4. hockey
5. tea	5. no	5. rear	5. no	5. yes	5. puppy
6. seat	6. yes	6. treat	6. flea	6. no	6. donkey
7. tear	7. yes	7. clean	7. ear	7. no	7. messy
8. heat	8. yes	8. meal	8. leap	8. yes	8. money
9. meat	9. no	9. cream	9. neat	9. yes	9. empty
10. seal	10. yes	10. scream	10. seat	10. yes	10. pokey

Page 83	Page 84	Page 85	Page 86	Page 87	Page 89
1. yes	1. hockey	1. no	1. study	1. yes	1. no
2. no	2. hilly	2. no	2. keys	2. no	2. no
3. no	3. honey	3. no	3. fussy	3. no	3. yes
4. no	4. kitty	4. yes	4. foggy	4. yes	4. no
5. no	5. turkey	5. yes	5. lazy	5. no	5. yes
6. no	6. lady	6. yes	6. penny	6. skinny	6. yes
7. yes	7. monkey	7. yes	7. messy	7. grumpy	7. no
8. no	8. lucky	8. no	8. whiskey	8. puppy	8. yes
9. yes	9. key	9. no	9. belly	9. messy	9. no
10. yes	10. happy	10. yes	10. rusty	10. turkey	10. yes

Page 90	Page 91	Page 92	Page 93	Page 94	Page 95
1. bite	1. no	1. tire	1. yes	1. bike	1. yes
2. fire	2. no	2. bite	2. no	2. kite	2. yes
3. ripe	3. yes	3. tile	3. yes	3. hive	3. yes
4. ride	4. yes	4. pipe	4. no	4. hike	4. no
5. tie	5. no	5. dive	5. no	5. pie	5. no
6. tire	6. yes	6. mine	6. yes	6. tired	6. bike
7. pipe	7. no	7. time	7. yes	7. hire	7. crime
8. sides	8. yes	8. wine	8. yes	8. wipe	8. smile
9. tile	9. no	9. dime	9. no	9. prize	9. die
10. pie	10. yes	10. bike	10. yes	10. lie	10. pipe

Page 97	Page 98	Page 99	Page 100	Page 101	Page 102
1. yes	1. fight	1. yes	1. night	1. yes	1. bright
2. no	2. light	2. yes	2. fright	2. yes	2. high
3. yes	3. high	3. no	3. high	3. yes	3. tight
4. no	4. right	4. yes	4. bright	4. no	4. fight
5. yes	5. bright	5. no	5. tight	5. yes	5. light
6. no	6. sigh	6. yes	6. sigh	6. no	6. sigh
7. yes	7. tight	7. yes	7. right	7. no	7. tights
8. yes	8. might	8. yes	8. night	8. yes	8. slight
9. yes	9. fright	9. no	9. fight	9. yes	9. night
10. no	10. night	10. yes	10. light	10. yes	10. sight

Page 103	Page 105	Page 106	Page 107	Page 108	Page 109
1. yes	1. no	1. fly	1. yes	1. fly	1. no
2. no	2. yes	2. sky	2. no	2. pry	2. yes
3. yes	3. no	3. dry	3. no	3. sky	3. yes
4. yes	4. no	4. why	4. no	4. fry	4. yes
5. yes	5. yes	5. fry	5. yes	5. cry	5. no
6. slight	6. yes	6. cry	6. yes	6. try	6. no
7. fight	7. yes	7. buy	7. yes	7. fly	7. no
8. light	8. no	8. guy	8. yes	8. by	8. no
9. right	9. no	9. pry	9. yes	9. dry	9. yes
10. might	10. no	10. fly	10. no	10. guy	10. yes

Page 110	Page 111	Page 113	Page 114	Page 115	Page 116
1. dry	1. no	1. yes	1. nose	1. yes	1. bone
2. guys	2. yes	2. yes	2. bone	2. yes	2. rose
3. try	3. yes	3. yes	3. joke	3. no	3. stone
4. fly	4. no	4. yes	4. poke	4. yes	4. Joe
5. cry	5. yes	5. no	5. hole	5. no	5. bone
6. dye	6. buy	6. no	6. woke	6. yes	6. hole
7. spy	7. try	7. no	7. pole	7. no	7. joke
8. sky	8. dry	8. no	8. rope	8. yes	8. toe
9. fry	9. sky	9. yes	9. rose	9. yes	9. rope
10. shy	10. guy	10. yes	10. sore	10. no	10. nose

Page 117	Page 118	Page 119	Page 121	Page 122	Page 123
1. yes	1. nose	1. yes	1. no	1. toast	1. no
2. yes	2. drove	2. no	2. no	2. soak	2. no
3. no	3. stove	3. yes	3. yes	3. soap	3. yes
4. yes	4. hole	4. no	4. no	4. boast	4. no
5. yes	5. toes	5. no	5. no	5. croak	5. yes
6. no	6. rose	6. bones	6. no	6. goat	6. yes
7. yes	7. joke	7. tore	7. yes	7. road	7. no
8. no	8. robe	8. smoke	8. yes	8. coat	8. yes
9. no	9. broke	9. robe	9. yes	9. toad	9. yes
10. yes	10. note	10. store	10. no	10. loan	10. yes

Page 124	Page 125	Page 126	Page 127	Page 128	Page 130
1. load	1. yes	1. road	1. no	1. yes	1. mow
2. boat	2. no	2. oars	2. no	2. no	2. bowl
3. coal	3. no	3. boast	3. no	3. no	3. grow
4. road	4. no	4. coat	4. yes	4. yes	4. blow
5. boast	5. no	5. float	5. no	5. no	5. low
6. goat	6. yes	6. goat	6. soap	6. no	6. crow
7. roar	7. no	7. soak	7. toast	7. yes	7. bowl
8. coat	8. yes	8. soap	8. boat	8. yes	8. snow
9. soap	9. yes	9. oats	9. coals	9. no	9. tow
10. toast	10. no	10. throat	10. coat	10. no	10. slow

Page 131	Page 132	Page 133	Page 134	Page 135	Page 137
1. no	1. snow	1. no	1. bowl	1. no	1. no
2. yes	2. row	2. yes	2. yellow	2. yes	2. no
3. yes	3. bowl	3. no	3. crow	3. no	3. yes
4. yes	4. bow	4. no	4. grown	4. yes	4. yes
5. yes	5. tow	5. no	5. blow	5. no	5. no
6. no	6. blow	6. yes	6. own	6. grow	6. no
7. no	7. bowl	7. yes	7. elbow	7. bow	7. no
8. yes	8. grow	8. no	8. snow	8. pillow	8. yes
9. yes	9. snow	9. yes	9. row	9. bowl	9. yes
10. no	10. mow	10. yes	10. pillow	10. elbows	10. yes

Page 138	Page 139	Page 140	Page 141	Page 142	Page 143
1. June	1. no	1. mule	1. no	1. fuel	1. yes
2. tune	2. no	2. fuel	2. no	2. glue	2. no
3. blue	3. yes	3. fumes	3. yes	3. tune	3. no
4. rule	4. no	4. glue	4. yes	4. huge	4. no
5. cure	5. yes	5. rude	5. no	5. puke	5. no
6. prune	6. no	6. June	6. yes	6. rule	6. clue
7. mule	7. yes	7. cure	7. yes	7. blue	7. blue
8. due	8. yes	8. Duke	8. no	8. mule	8. prune
9. glue	9. yes	9. huge	9. yes	9. June	9. fume
10. rude	10. yes	10. blue	10. yes	10. fumes	10. mule

Page 145	Page 146	Page 147	Page 148	Page 149	Page 150
1. no	1. fruit	1. yes	1. suit	1. yes	1. suit
2. yes	2. bruise	2. yes	2. fruit	2. yes	2. ruin
3. no	3. fruit	3. no	3. bruise	3. yes	3. juice
4. yes	4. juice	4. no	4. juice	4. no	4. fruit
5. yes	5. suit	5. yes	5. suit	5. yes	5. ruin
6. yes	6. juice	6. no	6. ruin	6. no	6. bruise
7. yes	7. cruise	7. no	7. juice	7. no	7. fruit
8. yes	8. ruin	8. no	8. bruise	8. no	8. cruise
9. yes	9. fruit	9. yes	9. fruit	9. yes	9. juice
10. no	10. suit	10. no	10. suit	10. no	10. suit

Page 151	Page 153	Page 154	Page 155	Page 156	Page 157
1. no	1. yes	1. shed	1. no	1. crash	1. yes
2. no	2. no	2. shop	2. yes	2. finish	2. yes
3. yes	3. yes	3. shot	3. yes	3. shrub	3. no
4. no	4. yes	4. dish	4. no	4. shelf	4. no
5. no	5. no	5. rush	5. yes	5. shot	5. no
6. fruit	6. yes	6. rash	6. yes	6. ship	6. yes
7. suit	7. yes	7. shell	7. yes	7. shock	7. no
8. bruise	8. no	8. fish	8. yes	8. crush	8. yes
9. ruin	9. yes	9. trash	9. no	9. flush	9. no
10. juice	10. yes	10. dash	10. no	10. hush	10. no

Page 158	Page 159	Page 161	Page 162	Page 163	Page 164
1. shrub	1. no	1. yes	1. mother	1. yes	1. bath
2. dish	2. no	2. yes	2. clothes	2. yes	2. path
3. relish	3. yes	3. no	3. brother	3. yes	3. throat
4. shrimp	4. no	4. yes	4. bathe	4. yes	4. thick
5. shred	5. no	5. yes	5. then	5. no	5. math
6. shall	6. cash	6. yes	6. those	6. yes	6. cloth
7. splash	7. shot	7. yes	7. them	7. yes	7. Beth
8. plush	8. splash	8. no	8. gather	8. yes	8. sixth
9. flesh	9. dish	9. yes	9. father	9. no	9. thin
10. shack	10. crash	10. yes	10. lather	10. no	10. moth

Page 165	Page 166	Page 167	Page 169	Page 170	Page 171
1. yes	1. both	1. no	1. no	1. rich	1. yes
2. yes	2. teeth	2. yes	2. yes	2. chill	2. yes
3. no	3. bath	3. no	3. no	3. champ	3. no
4. yes	4. cloth	4. yes	4. yes	4. punch	4. yes
5. no	5. think	5. no	5. yes	5. chips	5. no
6. no	6. throw	6. Beth	6. yes	6. chick	6. yes
7. yes	7. three	7. teeth	7. no	7. chin	7. yes
8. no	8. thick	8. throat	8. no	8. child	8. yes
9. yes	9. math	9. clothes	9. yes	9. pinch	9. no
10. yes	10. thin	10. think	10. no	10. lunch	10. no

Page 172	Page 173	Page 174	Page 175	Page 177	Page 178
1. catch	1. yes	1. chin	1. no	1. no	1. whale
2. witch	2. yes	2. porch	2. no	2. no	2. when
3. scratch	3. no	3. patch	3. no	3. no	3. whisper
4. hatch	4. yes	4. chose	4. no	4. yes	4. whiskers
5. Mitch	5. yes	5. hatchet	5. yes	5. yes	5. wheels
6. itch	6. yes	6. chubby	6. punch	6. yes	6. why
7. patch	7. yes	7. chat	7. match	7. yes	7. whistle
8. crutch	8. no	8. chase	8. lunch	8. no	8. whack
9. fetch	9. yes	9. cheat	9. witch	9. yes	9. whirl
10. match	10. no	10. fetch	10. scratch	10. yes	10. while

Page 179	Page 180	Page 181	Page 182	Page 183	Page 185
1. no	1. whine	1. no	1. whale	1. no	1. yes
2. yes	2. whisper	2. yes	2. whisper	2. yes	2. yes
3. no	3. whip	3. no	3. whisker	3. no	3. yes
4. yes	4. where	4. no	4. whirl	4. no	4. no
5. yes	5. whistle	5. yes	5. white	5. yes	5. no
6. yes	6. white	6. yes	6. whack	6. white	6. no
7. no	7. whale	7. yes	7. whiskey	7. whiskers	7. no
8. no	8. why	8. yes	8. whimper	8. when	8. yes
9. yes	9. whiskers	9. yes	9. wheat	9. whale	9. yes
10. yes	10. wheel	10. no	10. whoa	10. whack	10. no

Page 186	Page 187	Page 188	Page 189	Page 190	Page 191
1. alphabet	1. no	1. orphan	1. yes	1. elephant	1. yes
2. sphere	2. yes	2. trophy	2. yes	2. sphere	2. yes
3. graph	3. yes	3. nephew	3. no	3. phone	3. no
4. triumph	4. no	4. Joseph	4. yes	4. phonics	4. no
5. gopher	5. yes	5. phone	5. yes	5. dolphin	5. yes
6. phone	6. yes	6. physical	6. yes	6. photo	6. phone
7. nephew	7. yes	7. alphabet	7. yes	7. trophy	7. sphere
8. dolphin	8. yes	8. elephant	8. yes	8. gopher	8. Joseph
9. photos	9. no	9. asphalt	9. yes	9. Ralph	9. orphan
10. Ralph	10. yes	10. Phil	10. no	10. nephew	10. elephant

Page 193	Page 194	Page 195	Page 196	Page 197	Page 198
1. yes	1. car	1. yes	1. carry	1. yes	1. barn
2. no	2. jar	2. no	2. library	2. yes	2. carrot
3. yes	3. dark	3. yes	3. parrot	3. no	3. jar
4. yes	4. park	4. yes	4. carrot	4. yes	4. narrow
5. yes	5. star	5. no	5. marry	5. no	5. cart
6. yes	6. card	6. no	6. narrow	6. no	6. car
7. no	7. barn	7. no	7. parent	7. yes	7. marry
8. no	8. farm	8. no	8. arrow	8. yes	8. yard
9. yes	9. bark	9. yes	9. spare	9. yes	9. card
10. yes	10. arm	10. yes	10. scarce	10. no	10. arm

Page 199	Page 201	Page 202	Page 203	Page 204	Page 205
1. yes	1. yes	1. winner	1. yes	1. where	1. yes
2. no	2. yes	2. letter	2. yes	2. berry	2. yes
3. yes	3. yes	3. dinner	3. no	3. terrible	3. yes
4. yes	4. yes	4. sticker	4. yes	4. cherry	4. no
5. no	5. yes	5. never	5. yes	5. there	5. no
6. hard	6. yes	6. timer	6. no	6. Perry	6. yes
7. car	7. yes	7. paper	7. yes	7. berry	7. yes
8. arrow	8. no	8. summer	8. yes	8. merry	8. yes
9. stars	9. no	9. butter	9. yes	9. cherry	9. yes
10. carry	10. no	10. hammer	10. yes	10. where	10. yes

Page 206	Page 207	Page 209	Page 210	Page 211	Page 212
1. terrible	1. yes	1. yes	1. girl	1. no	1. bird
2. cherry	2. yes	2. yes	2. bird	2. yes	2. dirt
3. merry	3. yes	3. yes	3. dirt	3. yes	3. shirt
4. timer	4. yes	4. yes	4. third	4. yes	4. stir
5. sticker	5. yes	5. no	5. stir	5. no	5. thirty
6. pepper	6. cherry	6. yes	6. chirp	6. yes	6. skirt
7. camper	7. numbers	7. yes	7. skirt	7. yes	7. first
8. dinner	8. zipper	8. yes	8. firm	8. no	8. circle
9. summer	9. there	9. yes	9. twirl	9. no	9. sir
10. expert	10. letter	10 .yes	10. shirt	10. yes	10. Kirk

Page 213	Page 214	Page 215	Page 217	Page 218	Page 219
1. yes	1. dirt	1. no	1. yes	1. horse	1. no
2. no	2. shirt	2. yes	2. yes	2. porch	2. yes
3. yes	3. giraffe	3. yes	3. yes	3. corn	3. yes
4. no	4. thirty	4. no	4. no	4. sore	4. yes
5. no	5. girls	5. yes	5. no	5. cord	5. yes
6. no	6. squirt	6. sir	6. yes	6. fork	6. no
7. no	7. stir	7. third	7. yes	7. storm	7. no
8. no	8. circus	8. firm	8. yes	8. core	8. yes
9. yes	9. skirt	9. bird	9. yes	9. wore	9. yes
10. yes	10. flirt	10. dirt	10. yes	10. store	10. no

Page 220	Page 221	Page 222	Page 223	Page 225	Page 226
1. fork	1. yes	1. cord	1. no	1. yes	1. burp
2. cord	2. yes	2. ignore	2. no	2. yes	2. purse
3. snore	3. yes	3. forgot	3. no	3. yes	3. murder
4. porch	4. no	4. wore	4. yes	4. no	4. fur
5. wore	5. yes	5. snore	5. yes	5. yes	5. burn
6. short	6. no	6. horse	6. corn	6. no	6. nurse
7. chore	7. no	7. horn	7. chore	7. yes	7. burst
8. north	8. yes	8. corn	8. shore	8. yes	8. purple
9. tore	9. yes	9. storm	9. tore	9. yes	9. turn
10. corn	10. yes	10. sore	10. short	10. no	10. hurt

Page 227	Page 228	Page 229	Page 230	Page 231
1. no	1. purple	1. yes	1. purse	1. no
2. yes	2. turns	2. yes	2. hurts	2. no
3. no	3. turkey	3. no	3. fur	3. no
4. no	4. purr	4. no	4. nurse	4. yes
5. yes	5. nurse	5. yes	5. curls	5. yes
6. yes	6. hurt	6. no	6. murder	6. injure
7. no	7. purse	7. yes	7. burst	7. hurt
8. no	8. turn	8. no	8. burger	8. curls
9. no	9. curse	9. no	9. turkey	9. turkey
10. no	10. fur	10. no	10. burp	10. purse

Phonics Practice
Made Easy and Fun

Student Workbook B

Includes the following sounds or sound groupings:

Special Vowel Sounds, Digraphs, and Dipthongs

Short ea (as in h**ea**d)
ie, ei, and eigh (as in gr**ie**f, v**ei**n, sl**eigh** and dec**ei**t)
oi (as in **oi**l)
oy (as in b**oy**)
ow (as in **ow**l)
ou (as in **ou**t)
ough (as in th**ough**t, d**ough**, thr**ough**, r**ough**, c**ough**, b**ough**)
oo (as in z**oo** and b**oo**k)
aw (as in p**aw**)
au and augh (as in P**au**l and t**augh**t)
ew (as in n**ew** or m**ew**)
a (as in Am**a**nd**a**)
all and al sounded (as in w**all** and w**al**k)

Special Consonant Sounds and Combinations

nk (as in si**nk**)
ng (as in si**ng**)
Soft c (as in fa**c**e)
Soft g and dge (as in a**g**e and fu**dge**)
wr, kn, and mb (as in **wr**ap, **kn**ot and com**b**)
ch (as in **Ch**ris and **ch**ef)

W-Controlled Vowel Combinations

wa (as in **wa**sp)
war (as in **war**m and cow**ar**d)
wor (as in **wor**m)

Middles and Endings

ed (as in test**ed**, fix**ed**, and fri**ed**)
al and le (as in fin**al** and hand**le**)
tion and sion and cian (as in fic**tion**, ses**sion**, ver**sion**, and opti**cian**)
tive and sive (as in cap**tive** and cur**sive**)
ture, sure and su (as in pic**ture** and pres**sure**, trea**sure**, and **su**gar)